TO WHO
A COMPETITION FOR GLORY

AARON TREDWAY

To William —

Soli Deo Gloria

Printing provided by

www.FormaxPrinting.com

TO MY
FRIEND JON

❧

A true example *of a* life lived
for the glory of God

CONTENTS

PREGAME

PREGAME

It was a routine play.

I called for the ball, readied myself and jumped just like always.

Soaring through the crowd of players everything seemed fine – routine. I caught the ball like always. I began descending through the air as usual. I inadvertently prepared to land. Then it happened. Completely unexpected. Like a sniper awaiting the enemy during war.

I'll probably never know why it happened but it did. Nobody pushed me. Nobody nudged me. I don't think anyone even touched me. It was a routine play that would ultimately change my entire perspective on why I play the game – even more, on how I live my life.

A few days later I was approached by a pleasant woman in a white dress. She promptly asked me, "Can I get you something to eat or drink?" I hadn't formulated my order yet, but I figured I'd just play it safe and go for my usual, so asked her to get me a cinnamon crunch bagel and a skim vanilla latte.

A cinnamon crunch bagel and a skim vanilla latte.

Waiting for the waitress to retrieve my order I began to notice the bagel shop looked different that day.

The walls were oddly covered in white with no real effort made towards decoration.

Most of the customers were clothed in dress-like pajamas and there was no seating area, just beds.

It was just prior to my waitress's return that the anesthetic began to wear off. At that moment I made the shocking discovery – I wasn't in the bagel shop . . . I was at the hospital recovering from knee surgery!

The nurse and I had a good laugh when she brought me back half a glazed doughnut and a lemon-lime Gatorade.

SHIFTING PERSPECTIVE

Maybe you've had one of those "Ah ha!" moments too? One of those instances in life when formerly confusing things become clear?

Maybe an event that caused you to have a shift in perspective?

While I laid in the hospital recovering from that routine play gone wrong, that's exactly what happened to me.

A *shift* in **perspective**.

Given time to ponder life and my athletic career, I began to develop some very serious internal questions.

> *Why do I play?*
>
> *What is my objective as an athlete?*
>
> *How does my athletic career relate to the rest of my life?*
>
> *Am I making the most out of my athletic career?*

I began to wonder if there was something more. Something beyond my finite view of life and sport. Something bigger. Something Grander. Something more compelling than the ordinary reality I simply accepted as truth.

RUNNING TO WIN

As I lay in that hospital bed my thoughts roamed the varied experiences I'd accumulated over the years.

Ultimately my thoughts parked on Alex.

Alex was a warrior.

Alex kicked and scrapped and clawed and pulled the team to victory every week.

Alex was a leader.

Alex was team captain my first season as a professional soccer player. Because I was new to the team, Alex quickly took me under his wing and began imparting many years of professional soccer playing experience to me. I respected Alex.

But... while I respected Alex, I hated him at the same time.

Ok, I didn't really hate him, but I did profoundly dislike his leadership every Tuesday afternoon. Tuesday was team fitness day, and practice inevitably began with a 5-mile run. During the run Alex would always lead the way and shout back at the rest of the team, "This is your job, boys – enjoy it!"

How I hated Tuesdays!

For some reason Alex seemed to love practice just as much as he loved the game.

One Tuesday just before our team run I asked Alex why he liked running so much. I'll never forget his response – "I hate running on Tuesday but I love to win on Saturday!"

I hate running but I love winning.

In that moment my opinion of Tuesday afternoon was forever changed. Part of me celebrated that I wasn't alone in my disdain for running, but most of me focused on this radically altered perspective – *we run on Tuesday to win on Saturday.*

Up until that moment I had Tuesday all wrong. I thought Tuesday was a cruel joke imposed on players by management and the coaching staff; something to be endured, not appreciated.

Alex taught me an invaluable lesson: *If you want to win you've got to understand the game.*

A MICROCOSM OF LIFE

I've heard it said that sport is a microcosm of life.

One sporting event has the potential to contain many of the emotions, challenges, joys and tribulations we encounter in our everyday existence.

Think about it--whether you play forty, sixty, or ninety minutes, the multitude of experiences contained within that short time period is astonishing. One minute you're full of anticipation and expectation as the game is about to begin. Seconds later you could be pressed deep into your own half struggling to survive. Maybe your opponent throws you a cheap shot or slides in with a two-foot tackle and you burn with anger. Or maybe your team has been pressing for that much-needed goal and it finally comes in the last minute of the game sending you and your team into a euphoric state of celebration.

Whether you are a player or spectator, sport is a comprehensive life experience. That was well illustrated a few years ago by a T-shirt company that popularized the expression *Sport is life.* While I proudly wore my *Sport is life* T-shirt, broadcasting this mantra to all who would listen, I have actually come to believe sport is not life. Rather . . .

Sport is *like* life.

GRAND COMPETITION

Alex taught me that winning the game has everything to do with perspective; a clear understanding of Tuesday directly affects the outcome on Saturday.

Life is similar.

If sport is like life, I wonder, have you ever thought about life as a competition such as the World Cup of soccer?

At its core, the World Cup is a thirty-two-team tournament that is all about one nation emerging as the indisputable soccer champion of the world.

The World Cup is a competition.

Life is a competition too.

Whether we like it or not, athlete or spectator, we are all competing in this life. Competition is not really a choice, but the way we go about the competition is. The apostle Paul said this about the life-competition, "In a race everyone runs, but only one person gets the prize. Run to win"[1]

EVERYONE RUNS.

The good news about the "life race" is that we all can win. The choice is not whether or not we will enter the race, but choosing to "compete" in such a way as to win the prize.

I hope that's why you've picked up this book. Maybe it was given to you... Maybe you found it somewhere... Maybe it has just mystically appeared . . . whatever the case, this book is all about running in such a way as to win the prize. It's about the grand competition that we all participate in – the competition for glory.

VISION

I have come to believe that we have been designed to win, but winning is almost always a derivative of vision.

It's like the archer who seeks to hit the bull's-eye. If he's not aiming at the right target, the archer can hit the mark one hundred percent of the time and never win. Yet, having identified the correct target, and accurately aligning with that target, the archer can achieve unlimited success.

Look around.

We are all aimed at something.

Whether we like it or not, athlete or spectator, we are all competing.

The apostle Paul concluded his commentary on the race we all run in saying that some compete for a perishable crown, while others compete for a crown that is imperishable.

Victory in sport is important, but victory beyond sport is essential.

I hope this book will meet you on the path to victory and prove useful in the Grand Competition of life.

ONE

Grand Beginnings

ONE
Grand Beginnings

I like table tennis.

I do not like table tennis with Glen.

Let me explain.

Glen and I are competitors to the core. While we have been friends for many years, our friendship is characterized by competition. Whether on the soccer field, the tennis court, mini-hoops, or even Go Fish, Glen and I compete in just about everything.

We don't often play table tennis, but when we do it's all-out war. One evening Glen and I were engaged in an epic battle of skill, wit, and savvy. As I sat on the porch recovering, I remembered why I do not like table tennis with Glen. In fact, I remembered clearly why I do not like most any sport with Glen. It's because of a phrase Glen loves to repeat during competition.

Good guys 10, bad guys 7.

If Glen is losing the score changes, but the message remains the same.

Good guys 10, bad guys 14.

Either way, Glenn loves irritating his opponent with this simple little phrase.

I know, it's stupid. It shouldn't affect me. It's a silly, meaningless, ridiculous little expression . . . that absolutely drives me crazy!

Glen knows that. He loves that. And so he says it all the time.

Trained to Contend

The competition with Glen had concluded for that day, but exiting my driveway he heroically pronounced through the window of his blue '96 Honda Accord, "You won the battle, but the war continues!"

Whether he knew it or not, Glen had left me with a profound insight into life.

The war continues.

It's not my natural inclination to think of life as war, yet maybe life has more to do with war than I think.

As an athlete, my job description is competition.

The English word athlete finds its origins in ancient Greece. An athlete was an individual who was a contestant or prizefighter in the public games of ancient Greece or Rome, "one trained to contend in exercises requiring great physical agility and strength; a champion." [2]

Contestant or prizefighter, competition is sewn into the fabric of what it means to be an athlete.

Barring my fleeting desire to become Russell Crow in the Hollywood reenactment of the Battle of Carthage, I haven't often thought of myself as a gladiator, but that is exactly the original concept of an athlete.

Any person trained to contend.

This begs the question: trained to contend for what? Or against what?

Two Sides

My aversion to Glen's good guys/bad guys jeer reveals a deep-rooted ambivalence I feel towards the original description of an athlete. At the core of Glen's declaration we find opposition.

Good guys 10, bad guys 7.

Opposition.

Good guys 10, bad guys 14.

Opposition.

What makes Glen's team good and my team bad?

Why can't we both be the good team?

Maybe we are actually both the bad team??

Regardless, inherent in the competition we find the reality

of two sides. Like it or not, these two sides are at war. The impetus for this war may be varied, but the war is inevitable. Opposition exists.

In ancient Greece the verb athlein suggested a contest that culminated with a prize.[3] The ancients were not just competing, they were competing for something.

There was a goal, a tangible reward for efforts made. The object of the competition was the prize.

There is nothing to suggest that the original Greek athletes were inherently good or bad, but it is safe to conclude that competition was centered on opposition and the ultimate struggle was for a prize awarded to the victor.

Can you identify with the following description?

> An individual trained to compete against an
> opponent with purpose.

There was a term used by the ancients to describe this type of individual:

Athlete.

There is a similar term used today.

Athlete.[4]

Of course, culture has changed since then. Society has progressed. Times are different, but athletes remain.

While many centuries have passed between the original Greek sportsman and us, the concept remains. Sportsmen are those who choose to be trained in a particular discipline that they might ultimately compete against an opponent with purpose: for something.

Pretty simple, huh?

Few argue with this definition of an athlete, but many get stuck on the "for something." Of course athletes compete; it's part of the job description. But the prize athletes compete for… now that's the real debate.

FOR SOMETHING

A popular American professional basketball player recently commented:

> In my life I have won and accomplished much. I own three NBA championship rings. I've had plenty of endorsement deals and made a lot of money from them. But still, I feel as if I have yet to fulfill the blessing that God has given me in my ability to play this game. I feel as if there is so much more to do, on the court and off it. I don't know if this is how I am supposed to feel. Did MJ, Magic, and the others feel the same way? In our society it seems like athletes are expected to care about winning the game, pleasing the crowd, and signing deals. Period. But am I supposed to obsess myself with winning only to win, retire, and wonder if all my sacrifices were worth it?[5]

Here is an athlete who has everything; championship rings, endorsement deals, and enough money to live like royalty the rest of his life. He is accomplished, respected, and adored. Most athletes would trade a big toe to know the accomplishments of this guy. Yet, this question calls out from the inner most parts of his being: Why compete?

> Am I supposed to obsess myself with winning only to win?
>
> Why fight?
>
> Why struggle?
>
> Why sacrifice?
>
> What's the purpose?

Somewhere within us we all know the answer, don't we?

As my high school chemistry teacher used to say, "It's not rocket science!"

We compete . . . for something.

Something Else

While there may not be any official record of Jesus kicking a fifty-yard field goal or performing a flawless balance-beam routine, he knew a great deal about that something for which we all compete. Jesus once asked his closest friends, "What good would it do to get everything you want and lose the real you?"[6]

I think Jesus was suggesting there may be something else

besides all that we usually esteem as something. Let's call this something else the real you.

Jesus hung out with a pretty rough crowd— maybe not so different from some of the other players on your team, or the sportsmen you watch on television. The religious leaders of Jesus' day ridiculed him for his choice of friends. Jesus didn't care, he knew his purpose. He knew his "real you."

Jesus knew who he was because he knew his purpose. The good news is that we can know our purpose too.

A man named Paul encountered Jesus on his way to a town called Damascus. That brief encounter changed Paul's entire perspective on who he really was; Paul encountered his real you.

Following that encounter with Jesus, Paul spent the rest of his life traveling the world with one overarching mission, to proclaim his Damascus-road revelation: "There is only one God, the Father, who created everything, and we exist for him."[7]

We exist . . . for him.

Wait a second. What about the money? What about the rings? What about the endorsement deals, the adoration, the popularity, and the fame?

As an athlete, don't I exist for these things?

Don't get me wrong, these things may be important; we may even need (or think we need) some of these things, but they are not the real you. In fact, these things often wage war with and threaten to steal the real you.

In an effort to communicate the real you to people in Colossae (a city in what is now modern-day Turkey), Paul wrote, "For everything, absolutely everything, above and below, visible and invisible, rank after rank after rank of angels— everything got started in him and finds its purpose in him."[8]

Paul makes it pretty clear, the real you is all about Jesus. Yet, for most of us, this presents a quandary; my real you is found in him, but I'm all about me.

I want the rings, the money, the endorsement deals, the adoration, the popularity, and the fame for me, but God wants it all for himself. And so we encounter what I call the Grand Competition, the competition for glory–my glory versus God's glory.

Never Trust a Snake

The Grand Competition is not a new competition; it finds its origins all the way back at the beginning of mankind.

The "book of beginnings," Genesis, records God's creation of human beings. "So God created people in his own image; God patterned them after himself; male and female he created them."[9]

We were created by God to be like God. We were created to exist in harmony with God and work towards the same goal—God's glory.

There was originally no competition between God and the creatures he made in his image; we existed in perfect unity with God . . . until we met the snake.

One day the first people, Adam and Eve, were walking their estate when they encountered the snake. In the movies this is the part where the eerie music starts up. The snake was said to be "the shrewdest of all creatures"[10] and crafty to no end.

The snake engaged Adam and Eve in a discussion and ultimately convinced them to do the one thing God had told them not to do—eat from a certain tree growing in their garden.

This single act of rebellion began the Grand Competition that continues today.

Our unity with God was broken; our formerly shared objective, God's glory, became the overwhelming object of contention.

You can think of this sudden loss of a shared objective as the start of a new game. Paul told us that God created everything for Himself—everything and everyone was originally a part of his game. Unfortunately for us, Adam and Eve weren't satisfied with the parameters of God's game and so they created their own.

Let's try and put this in perspective.

God created the grandest, most important, coolest game of all games, like the Super Bowl, Rugby World Cup Final,

NBA Finals, and World Cup of soccer all rolled into one—and Adam and Eve decided to take their ball and play elsewhere.

Adam and Eve's decision didn't stop God's Game of All Games from proceeding as planned; it simply opened the door for a choice. Whereas the original people were automatically selected as players in the Grand Game for God's glory, we now have the lamentable, yet very real option to choose to play in the smallest, most insignificant little game for our own glory instead. The choice is now ours.

Kabod

Glory can be a difficult concept.

The English definition is ambiguous at best: "Very great praise, honor, or distinction bestowed by common consent; renown."[11] As it pertains to the Grand Competition for glory, our English definition simply does not suffice.

The ancient Jewish prophets and teachers had some interesting insights about glory. The prophet Isaiah had a vision of angels proclaiming the glory of God. In his vision the angels were shouting, "Holy, holy, holy is the Lord Almighty; the whole earth is full of his glory."[12]

The Hebrew word used for glory is *kabod*, meaning weight or significance.

Commenting on the Hebrew use of the word glory, one writer notes the prophet's profound understanding of the condition of the universe: "The whole earth is full of the weight and significance of who God is."[13]

The glory of God is the weight and significance of who God is!

The angels exist to shout and proclaim the significance of God.

You and I were created for the same purpose, to proclaim the significance of God.

Yet the Adam-initiated alternative exists as well. The creation of the little pick-up game for our own glory strangely compels us. While everything was created by God and for God, in order that God's "weight and significance" might be proclaimed, we love our own kabod, don't we?

We love to proclaim the weight and significance of who we are, and that directly conflicts with who God is. Speaking through the prophet Isaiah, God said, "How can I let myself be defamed? I will not yield my glory to another."[14]

God loves to be glorified.

God loves to be glorified so much that he is unwilling to share his glory with anyone or anything else.

Shortly after Adam initiated the competition for glory, many people began thinking their personal significance was more important than God's. Genesis, the first book of the bible, speaks of the masses gathering to construct a royal city with an enormous tower at its center. As the people gathered, they said to one another, "Come, let us build ourselves a city, with a tower that reaches to the heavens, so that we may make a name for ourselves. . . ."[15]

So we may make a name for ourselves.

From antiquity human beings have conspired to make a name for themselves. We rationalize and think:

It's normal, everyone's out for number one!

Maybe so, but how does that affect the real you? How does that affect the person made for the glory of God? How does that affect the individual fashioned by God and for God to proclaim God's weight and significance?

Training to Contend for the Real You

Athletes are individuals who welcome challenge and embrace opposition.

Athletes love to compete.

Athletes don't just love to compete, they love to compete for something; a prize.

The resounding cultural message spoken to athletes is that competition is all about ME; it's about the number of championships I can win, the amount of popularity I can acquire, the size to which I can grow my bank account.

Yes, occasionally it's about the team; the number of championships the team can win, the amount of popularity the team can acquire, the amount of money the team can make.

Regardless, athletes are people trained to contend . . . for something. It's part of our inherent disposition.

"What good would it do to get everything you want and lose the real you?" Jesus asked. The question is just as applicable today as it was two thousand years ago.

> What good would it do to get everything you want and lose the real you?

The real you is all about kabod.

You exist to make known the significance of God: to display his grandeur, his magnificence, his wonder, his awesomeness, his glory.

With one voice the angels shout, "Holy, holy, holy is the Lord Almighty; the whole earth is full of his glory."[16]

You were made to do the same.

An individual in training to contend for glory— that is the real you, and glory is the ultimate prize.

As Glen reminded me after that battle of table tennis, "The war continues!"

We might not always play table tennis, but competition will always compel us.

TWO
Something More

TWO
Something More

How do you feel about rollerblading? Some of my teammates like to tease me about it. I don't care. I love it.

A few years ago I was hanging out with a teammate in the Anaheim hills near Los Angeles, California. The Anaheim hills are no Mt. Kilimanjaro, but they are not exactly flat either.

Benji had never been rollerblading, but he figured that if I could do it he could do it. After several days of debate we found a sports store and bought Benji his first pair of rollerblades. It was all *downhill* from there.

Benji is a goalkeeper. When you consider the characteristics of a goalkeeper you may think of words like courageous, fearless, brave, and bold. Generally, I've come to believe that you can explain a goalkeeper with just one word: CRAZY!

I will never forget that afternoon. What happened that day will forever live in the annals of locker room banter and rollerblading folklore.

I had no idea it was possible. I saw it with my own eyes and I still wonder if I really saw what I did.

In typical Benji (goalkeeper) fashion, he took off down the first of two large hills. I had not taught him how to stop at that point so, conquering the first hill, Benji rolled straight towards the second. That's when it happened. Benji's skates began shaking wildly and he lost control. Moments later Benji was airborne. BANG, he hit the street and bounced. BOOM, he hit the street again. BAM, BAM, BAM, he skipped across the hot mid-day asphalt and then came to a rolling halt.

Of course we neglected to buy safety equipment thinking, "We're athletes, what's the worst thing that could happen?"

It was the worst sporting accident I had ever witnessed. Benji lay lifeless as I quickly shed my rollerblades and ran towards him. Just as I arrived at the scene Benji miraculously sprang to his feet and proclaimed, "I'm good to go, Buddy!"

Benji was NOT *good to go.*

He was clearly in shock, as most of his body now had intimate knowledge of the black tar which constituted the street. Benji kept repeating, "I'm good to go Buddy . . . I'm good to go," in his distinct Kentucky accent. Then I saw it. (If you have a weak stomach please feel free to skip this part)

Ok, rather, I didn't see it.

Somewhere in between the bang, boom and bam, Benji

lost a nipple. That's right, gone. Right nipple fine. Left nipple nowhere to be found!

I looked everywhere for that nipple; couldn't find it.

Benji spent the next few days in the hospital recovering. I never found the nipple but oddly enough, about a year later it grew back.

GOOD TO GO

Benji is not so different from you and me. Ok, maybe we have both nipples intact, but like Benji, most of us think we are good to go most of the time. We maintain that all is well. Life is good. Things just couldn't be better.

Especially athletes.

Athletes are supposed to be strong, brave, courageous, and conquering. Anything less is culturally unacceptable.

Athletes are warriors -- individuals trained to contend against opposition for a prize.

Athletes are often likened to the gladiators of ancient Rome. Of course, all athletes are *good to go*. Things just couldn't be better.

What do you think?

Do you really believe that "things just couldn't be better?"

Isn't there something that cries out from the inner recesses of your being for something more? Something bigger?

Something grander? Something beyond our average everyday experience?

There was once a powerful king named Solomon who grappled with the same questions. Solomon was thought to be one of the wisest people of all time, and towards the end of his life he wrote his son Rehoboam a letter about the experiences he had as king.

Solomon wrote, "I said to myself, 'Look, I am wiser than any of the kings who ruled in Jerusalem before me. I have greater wisdom and knowledge than any of them.' So I worked hard to distinguish wisdom from foolishness. But now I realize that even this was like chasing the wind."[17]

CHASING THE WIND.

Solomon was searching for something more. Something better. Something deeply and profoundly more significant than his average consumer-driven life.

Solomon's entire life was devoted to this search. His letter to Rehoboam said that he did not withhold from himself anything he desired.[18] He was regarded as the greatest and most powerful ruler ever, yet Solomon was not content.

THE BALL

Yesterday I had lunch with two former teammates. It was a perfect fall day. Not too hot, not too cold. The leaves of the surrounding trees were boldly proclaiming the glory of the season; vibrant red, yellow and orange hues illuminated by the noon-day sun were surrounding us at all corners.

Just as I was devouring the final bite of my cosmic sub, Dana said, "I always loved the ball but it never loved me back."

Prior to this comment we had been discussing the discontentment each of us has felt at certain times of life. We all had a similar story. Each of us grew up with an overwhelming preoccupation; *sports*. Ultimately, each of us pursued one sport beyond the others, but sport in general still consumed us.

To suggest that sport was a preoccupation is to put it mildly; the ball meant everything to us. While we may have had other friends throughout our formative years, no one could compete with *the ball*. We gave all we had to *the ball*. We sacrificed time, sleep, friends, and family. We gave our lives for *the ball*.

Can you relate?

As each of us progressed in our sport the ball began to offer a certain amount of reciprocity; it began to give something back to us.

At first the ball offered acceptance; acceptance grew into notoriety, and notoriety ultimately became popularity. One day the ball became a passport. A passport is a document of identification; it tells the world who you are.

Dana shared about how the ball took him to many countries, introduced him to influential people, and even got him into parties. Just as we were concluding that we should be in debt to the ball for all it had given us, Dana said:

I always loved the ball but it never loved me back.

The ball gave much to each of us but it could not satisfy our deepest longing; we long for something profoundly more significant than the sum of who we are, the glory of our own existence. We inherently long for the glory of God.

Solomon wrote, "He [God] set eternity in the hearts of men."[19]

Inherent within the very composition of man is God. We long for God because we were fashioned with a void which only he can fill.

You were made for God!

Solomon's father David was king before him. In a poem about God, David wrote, "As the deer pants for streams of water, so I long for you, O God."[20]

David was an athlete in his youth. His talent with a slingshot ultimately earned him notoriety and respect (remember Goliath, the 10-foot warrior David defeated with just a stone and a sling shot?). Though David was elevated to the highest place of authority, wealth, and significance, he longed for something more than the sum of who he was; *he longed for God, just as God longed for him.*

That is the difference.

We love the ball and it has much to offer, but the ball

does not long for us; it does not love us back.

The ball does not miss us when we neglect it; it does not get angry when we avoid it.

The ball and all it has to offer are finite creations; God is the infinite Creator who created us to long for him just as he longs for us.

A popular 17th century French philosopher once commented, "There is a God shaped vacuum in the heart of every man which cannot be filled by any created thing, but only God, the creator, made known through Jesus."[21]

It's sort of like that popular children's game with the shapes. There is a star, a square, a triangle and a circle. Every shape has a corresponding hole in the circular plastic contraption. It's always entertaining to watch children attempting to press square shapes into triangular holes--it just doesn't fit.

That's what the French philosopher was saying, and what Dana discovered as well; no matter how hard you try, you cannot press square shapes into triangular holes; they just don't *fit*.

In the same way, there is a hole in your heart that only God can fill. Trying to press anything else apart from God into that hole won't work; it just doesn't fit.

Though King Solomon told his son Rehoboam he felt like he was "chasing the wind" for most of his life, he ultimately concluded that no one will find joy, contentment, purpose, or peace of mind of any enduring sort apart from God.[22]

The ball has much to offer but it can never fill your God-shaped hole. Money, notoriety, championship rings, and success are all wonderful by-products of the ball, but they can't fill the hole either.

MASTERPIECE

Have you ever thought of yourself as a painting?

The apostle Paul tells us, "We are God's masterpiece." This is taken from the Jewish concept of construction; *to create or bring forth*. Paul continued in saying, "He has created us anew in Christ Jesus, so we can do the good things he planned for us long ago." [23]

God created you with foresight; he began with the end in mind.

The Jewish prophet Jeremiah made this declaration on behalf of God: "I know what I'm doing. I have it all planned out."[24] Jeremiah originally made this declaration through a letter written to people who were about to be persecuted for 70 years. Try and imagine what those people must have been thinking . . . "God forgot about us!" "We are doomed!" "God doesn't care what happens to us!" God said quite the contrary – "I know what I'm doing. I have it all planned out."

Jeremiah wrote to tell the people that God is concerned

about their wellbeing and he DOES *have a plan* for their success; his plans are to *profit you.*

I don't know what the Jewish exiles thought, but I think that's pretty awesome. That means that God is working for me and not against me. God wants to see me prosper; he wants to see me succeed! Yet, the ultimate prosperity Jeremiah declared is all about the Hebrew word SHALOM.

Shalom means *peace* in English.

The Jewish recipients of Jeremiah's letter would have understood that God was declaring his desire for them to know peace beyond anything else in life. In ancient Jewish culture, peace was the equivalent of wholeness, and wholeness could only be found in God. Thus, Jewish listeners would have understood that God was declaring his abiding passion for their wholeness, and it was available only in himself.

In essence Jeremiah declared: *God knows the plans he has for you, plans to see you come to wholeness in Himself.*[25]

When God created you as his masterpiece, his ultimate objective was for you to know wholeness because of who he is. Without him, you are like Solomon--you can find yourself chasing after the wind and miss the real you.

UNIQUE

Remember: The *real you* is all about *him.*

There was no ambiguity in the board room the day God

brought forth the blueprints for your life. God knew exactly what he was creating and his purpose in creating you.

Comparing God's creative process to a business meeting, one author writes, "God's staff meetings, if he had them, would revolve around one question: 'How can we reveal my glory today?' God's to-do list consists of one item: 'Reveal my glory.' Heaven's framed and mounted purpose statement hangs in the angels' break room just above the angel food cake. It reads: 'Declare God's glory.'"[26]

God loves God's glory. Subsequently, all of creation--you, me, sports and everything else--exists to declare God and to make known his significance.

This presents a problem when compared to the resounding cultural message spoken to athletes today; It's all about me. It's about the number of championships I can win, the amount of popularity I can acquire, and the amount I can accumulate in my bank account. Yet, at the same time we long for something more, don't we?

We long for the glory of God.

We were created to compete for God's glory, but we live in a ME-centered world in which our personal glory is inevitably at odds with God's. This might not be our intention, but this is the Grand Competition that we have been discussing.

The Grand Competition has little to do with me versus you, or my team versus your team. Rather, the grand competition, the competition for the real you, comes down to my glory against God's. It's an epic battle royal for ultimate significance.

Do I compete to make MY significance known, or do I compete to declare that God is more significant than all other things?

Speaking through the Jewish prophet Isaiah, God said: "Bring my sons from afar and my daughters from the end of the earth, everyone who is called by my name, whom *I created for my glory.*"[27]

It's no mystery why God created you – it's all about him!

God created us for God because God loves God's glory.

God created sports for God because God loves God's glory.

God loves to use us in sports for God because . . . *you guessed it* . . . God loves God's glory!

A friend of mine likes to remind me, "You're unique just like everyone else." It's true. God created us each unique and special. We are his masterpiece and the object of his greatest affection. We have our own unique gifts and talents, and we have been created to have significance – *just like everyone else!*

As an athlete you might take offense at this suggestion. Athletes are often part of a team, but they love individuality at the same time. Athletes want the team to succeed but they also want their performance to uniquely contribute. This is not wrong. This is part of the way God made you – unique, just like everyone else.

The real you is an individual that uniquely competes for the team.

I've heard it said that "the team is only as strong as its weakest link." On a team everyone has a role to fill. From the star of the team to the last person on the bench, the team is only as strong as its weakest link. While the team is comprised of many unique individuals, the objective of the team is the same.

There are many motivational forces that drive an athlete; the coach, the fans, parents, friends and peers. Sometimes fear drives an athlete. Some athletes are motivated by potential reward. Regardless, athletes find success when the team they compete for is ultimately successful.

What team do you compete for?

Maybe you compete for your community team. Maybe you compete for your high school or college team. Maybe you are a professional athlete and you compete for a professional franchise. The truth is that God created you to compete for him.

Did you know that God loves you in sports?

It's true.

God loves you in sports because he loves YOU.

Jesus wanted the world to know about his Father's love and so he said: "This is how much God loved the world: he gave his Son, his one and only Son. And this is why: so that no one need be destroyed."[28]

God also loves you in sports because he loves his glory.

Paul tells us something about God's passion for us in sports: "Whether you eat or drink or whatever you do, do it all for the glory of God."[29]

Did you catch that?

WHATEVER *YOU DO . . .*

God is passionate about you in sports because he is passionate about you and his glory in *whatever* you do.

The real you does whatever you do for the glory of God; to declare God's significance.

This makes the real you unique, just like everyone else.

NAME

As I write this book I'm a single, 30-something, professional athlete and I watch Disney movies. Don't laugh, if you saw how cute my nieces are you would watch Disney movies too!

The other day Sakari (age 4) asked if we could watch her favorite movie together; *The Prince of Egypt.* Considering I'm currently in the running for uncle of the year, I committed my next 2 hours to the magical world of Disney.

Sakari loved the movie; she sang all the songs, danced like pharaoh, and even mimicked her favorite character's voice. Apparently twenty minutes of Disney was all Sakari could handle. She was off to dreamland before Moses had celebrated his first birthday!

So there I was, a single, 30-something, professional athlete watching *The Prince of Egypt* . . . alone.

Have you seen *The Prince of Egypt?* It turns out to be a compelling biography of a real life guy called Moses. Moses was a Hebrew born at the wrong time in history. He was born in Egypt at a time when the Egyptian ruler (Pharaoh) had issued a decree to kill all new-born Hebrew boys.

Moses' mother knew Moses was special, so she placed her new-born son in a basket and sent him down the Nile River, praying God would take care of him. He was found by Pharaoh's daughter and subsequently grew up as Egyptian royalty, only to learn later in life that he was actually a Hebrew.

God had a plan for Moses.

Moses was God's masterpiece; created unique and special – just like everyone else. He was a prince of Egypt but God planned something more.

One day God appeared to Moses through a burning bush in the desert. Forty years earlier Moses had realized he was a Hebrew, killed an Egyptian guard, and fled to a desert town called Midian. Moses had resolved to spend the rest of his days watching sheep; God had other plans, *something more.*

Moses' story is recorded in the Old Testament book of Exodus. Exodus says:

> God called to him from out of the bush, "Moses! Moses!" He said, "Yes? I'm right here!" God

said, "Don't come any closer. Remove your
sandals from your feet. You're standing on holy
ground." Then he said, "I am the God of your
father: The God of Abraham, the God of Isaac,
the God of Jacob." Moses hid his face, afraid to
look at God. God said, "I've taken a good, long
look at the affliction of my people in Egypt. I've
heard their cries for deliverance from their slave
masters; I know all about their pain. And now I
have come down to help them, pry them loose
from the grip of Egypt, get them out of that
country and bring them to a good land with
wide-open spaces, a land lush with milk and
honey, the land of the Canaanite, the Hittite,
the Amorite, the Perizzite, the Hivite, and the
Jebusite. The Israelite cry for help has come to
me, and I've seen for myself how cruelly they're
being treated by the Egyptians. It's time for
you to go back: I'm sending you to Pharaoh to
bring my people, the People of Israel, out of
Egypt." Moses answered God, "But why me?
What makes you think that I could ever go to
Pharaoh and lead the children of Israel out of
Egypt?" "I'll be with you," God said. "And this
will be the proof that I am the one who sent

you: When you have brought my people out
of Egypt, you will worship God right here at
this very mountain." Then Moses said to God,
"Suppose I go to the People of Israel and I tell
them, 'The God of your fathers sent me to you';
and they ask me, 'What is his name?' What do I
tell them?" God said to Moses, "I-AM-WHO-I-
AM. Tell the People of Israel, 'I-AM sent me to
you.' "[30]

Did you catch what just happened to Moses?

God invited Moses to compete for glory!

Moses was hanging out with his sheep in the desert
when God announced from a burning bush that he had
something more. Something **BIGGER**. Something **GRANDER**.
Something **LARGER** than Moses' everyday experience.

God told Moses that he had seen the plight of his
suffering people and he had a plan; he would rescue his people,
and he would use Moses to do it.

Moses answered God, "But why me?"

Moses knew who he was. He had spent almost eighty
years of his life competing in the smallest, most insignificant,
tiny, little pick-up game for his own glory. Though something
more had always called out to him, Moses had contented
himself with himself.

God knew who Moses was too.

Moses was worried that he wouldn't be influential enough to speak with Pharaoh; he was concerned by his own insignificance. And that was the point!

God invited Moses to be something more than the sum of who he was.

God invited Moses to something profoundly more significant than the glory of his own existence.

God invited Moses to compete in *WHATEVER YOU DO* for the glory of God.

God said to Moses, "I-AM-WHO-I-AM. Tell the People, 'I-AM sent me to you.'"

Can you imagine what Moses must have been thinking?

"What . . . *I-AM-WHO-I-AM?*" "That's never going to work, God!" "What's that supposed to mean, 'I-AM sent me to you?!'"

Commenting on Moses' story, one author suggests that when God told Moses that his name is "I-AM," he simultaneously told Moses his name as well. You see, if God's name is I-AM that only leaves one option for Moses, "I-AM-NOT."[31]

The same is true for you and me.

If God is I-AM, that only leaves one option for us -- I-AM-NOT!

Athletes are supposed to be strong, brave, courageous and conquering.

Athletes are warriors.

Athletes are often likened to the gladiators of ancient Rome, but athletes are not God.

Sometimes athletes are treated like gods (small "g"). Sometimes people see athletes as gods. Sometimes athletes even think they are gods, but they are not GOD.

God is I-AM. That means I-AM-NOT.

But, he invites you to compete for something more than the sum of your significance. You are invited to compete for God's glory in whatever you do.

SUPERHERO

For most of us, especially athletes, the reality that I-AM-NOT is hard to stomach. It might not always be an outward admission, but most athletes maintain their name is I-AM.

Athletes have been enculturated to believe that they are similar to superheroes. In fact, I'd be willing to place a bet that at some point in your life you had a degree of fascination with superman.

Superman represents characteristics that all athletes aspire to have. Superman is strong, fast, courageous and fearless. He fights for the good of mankind and seems impossible to defeat. Superman is superhuman. Athletes like that.

Superman is a personal favorite of mine, but he threatens to keep you from something more.

You may not be aware of this but many Bible passages could be seen as promoting a superman mentality.

"**I can do all things** through Him who strengthens me."[32]

"**We are more than conquerors** through him who loved us."[33]

Through him "**we will do mighty things**, for he will trample down our foes."[34]

Athletes love these verses because they evoke superhuman confidence; *I can do all things, we are more than conquerors, we will do mighty things.*

A popular Adidas slogan asserts, "Impossible is nothing." I agree, but sometimes we miss the point and overlook the source of our superhuman potential.

THROUGH HIM.

God invites you to compete for his glory *THROUGH HIM.*

It's through him you can do all things; through him we are more than conquerors, through him you can do mighty things.

It's THROUGH HIM and so it should be TO HIM.

HEAVEN'S EYES

The other day I was thinking about the movie night with Sakari. I don't want to make a habit of watching Disney movies alone, but one song in particular sticks out in my mind.

As the movie characters sang and danced, Sakari sang and danced along with them:

> *You must look at your life through heaven's*
> *eyes . . . though you might not know all the*
> *steps you must learn to join the dance.*

This seems like a pretty profound idea for a Disney movie!

If God is who God says he is, and God created you for the purpose he says he created you for, what do you think God sees when he looks at your life?

HIS GLORY!

You were created in the image of God to display God's image. God created you with a plan and a purpose to proclaim himself.

This may seem egotistical of God -- but think of yourself as a painting.

If you were to visit an art gallery where the greatest paintings ever created were housed, you could spend all day in awe of these great works of art. You would delight yourself in the brilliance of the paintings, giving praise and glory to their splendor. The paintings' grandeur warrants praise, but ultimate adoration can only be received by the painter himself. It's the creator, not the created, that deserves the glory.

You are *God's* masterpiece!

The real you was created for *something more.*

The *real you* was created for something much **BIGGER**, much **GRANDER**, much **LARGER**, and profoundly more significant than the sum of your personal existence.

The *real you* was created for the glory of God.

What do you think?

Are you *good to go?*

᠎᠎ꙮ

THREE

The Undisputed Heavyweight
Champion of the World

THREE

The Undisputed Heavyweight Champion of the World

Do you know Robert Knievel? Robert is his given name but most people call him "Evel" – EVEL KNIEVEL that is!

Just in case you've spent the past seventy years living in an underground nuclear bomb shelter in Outer Mongolia, I'll fill you in. Robert "Evel" Knievel is to extreme sports as Jordan is to basketball, Tiger is to golf, Pele is to soccer or Schumacher is to Formula One. He's the real deal!

Knievel was born October 17, 1938 in Butte, Montana. Raised by his grandparents, Knievel dropped out of high school after his sophomore year and proceeded to attempt vocations ranging from diamond drill operator to minor league professional hockey player. Seeking fame and fortune, Robert Knievel turned to motorcycles in the mid-1960s and formed a stunt team called *Evel Knievel and His Motorcycle Daredevils*.

Evel Knievel became a household name; he was a *daredevil.*

Initially Knievel attempted to jump over animals and pools of water, but several other stunt men were doing the same act. Knievel decided he needed to distinguish himself, so he began attempting to jump over vehicles.

Nothing seemed too *grand* a feat for Evel Knievel. Not even the ***Grand* Canyon**.

For years Evel Knievel told his fans he would jump the Grand Canyon on his motorcycle, but the United States government would never allow it. Flying home from a performance, Knievel looked out the window and saw the Snake River Canyon near Twin Falls, Idaho – he committed to jump it instead. Knievel set his historic jump date for September 8, 1974. Despite the creation of a rocket propelled "skycycle" and two failed test jumps, Knievel refused to disappoint his fans.

At 3:36pm on September 8, 1974, Evel Knievel stared directly into the face of opposition -- and lost. While his skycycle made it all the way across the canyon, the three ¼-inch bolts holding the cover of his parachute ripped off during the initial force of the blast, prematurely deploying the chute and pulling Knievel down into the immense canyon.

Knievel was defeated.

INVINCIBLE

At the height of Knievel's popularity he seemed invincible.
A friend of mine confessed that he loved Knievel because he
"defied death and lived to tell the story." There are numerous
books, a few movies (coolest of all *Viva Knievel*) and the
gratuitous Evel Knievel action figure (of which I had two).

Speaking about his unique approach to life, Knievel once
commented, "A Roman general in the time of Caesar had a
motto – 'If it is possible, it is done. If it is impossible... it will be
done.' And that, ladies and gentlemen, is what I live by."[35]

People loved Knievel because he represented all that is
bold, daring, and fearless about the human experience. Knievel
was a spokesman for humanity. A herald of man's indomitable
spirit. One friend of mine loved Knievel so much that she
would dress her schnauzer up in a red, white and blue jump
suit and coerce him to perform death-defying stunts in her
backyard.

Knievel was called arrogant, haughty, and cavalier
amongst other names. Regardless, he was revered as triumphant,
until Snake River Canyon, that is.

Snake River Canyon was the beginning of the end for
Evel Knievel. Sure, he still performed following that jump.
He still attempted death-defying stunts. He still represented
all of the same qualities and characteristics that had caused
many to call him "invincible," **BUT** now we knew he was not.

We probably knew it all along, but Evel Knievel captured the human imagination and provided a generation with the belief that man always wins.

King Solomon wrote, "First pride, then the crash – the bigger the ego, the harder the fall."[36] Stated another way, "Pride comes before the fall."

PRIDE. It's not necessarily a bad word.

You can be *proud* of someone or something. You can *proudly* display something. You might even see a *pride* of lions roaming in the jungle. But the pride Solomon refers to is pride of self; an "inordinate opinion of one's own dignity, importance, merit, or superiority."[37]

First pride, then the crash. That's what happened to Evel Knievel.

Knievel made a career out of crashing, but it wasn't until Snake River Canyon that people saw *the real you.* Knievel crashed so many times that he once commented, "There are a lot of myths about my injuries. They say I have broken every bone in my body. Not true. But I have broken 35 bones. I had surgery 14 times to pin and plate. I shattered my pelvis. I forget all of the things that have broke."[38] Evel Knievel was not invincible; neither is the real you.

SHEEP

Jesus asked his friend, "What good would it do to get everything you want and loose the real you?"[39]

Who is *the real you* anyway?

Would it really be so bad if I decided to forfeit *the real me* and do my own thing? If I forfeit the real me who will know; who will care?

These are all good questions. Normal questions. Questions that demand answers if *the real you* is to emerge and prove victorious.

I believe that just like you, whether he acknowledged it or not, Evel Knievel longed for something more than the sum of who he was; he longed for God because God longed for him.

The real you is the person that God created you to be. You are special, unique, gifted and endowed with immeasurable talent – *for God*.

God created you but He also gave you free will; you have the ability to choose who you will be and how you will live. Some people think that was a "rookie mistake" on God's part, but amongst other things, would God really receive glory if He forced you to live for Him?

A popular Christian author often says, "God is glorified in us when we are satisfied in him . . . the essence of worship is being satisfied in God."[40] The point is that God is glorified (shown more significant than everything else) when we are content in Him.

Culture has a funny way of diverting our priorities; this is the nature of the grand competition for glory. On one side there's God. God tells us, "I have raised you up, that I might show my power in you, and that my name might be proclaimed in all the earth."[41] On the other side there's me. Commenting on the universal condition of man, the prophet Isaiah compared us to sheep following our own path. Isaiah said, "All of us have strayed away like sheep. We have left God's paths to follow our own."[42]

Admittedly, our own paths are pretty cool, even fulfilling for a time, but they are not sustainable. You don't believe me? Ask Evel Knievel.

There was a guy in the Bible who had seen a fair bit in his life. Reflecting on the universal experience he had taken part in, John wrote, "The world and all its wanting, wanting, wanting is on the way out—but whoever does what God wants is set for eternity."[43]

So there we have it -- the key to unlocking *the real you*. If the real you is the person that God created you to be, and the person that does what God wants is "set for eternity," then the real question is – *what does God want?*

For the answer to this all important question you need look no further than King Nebuchadnezzar of Babylon.

BIG GOD SMALL ME

Nebuchadnezzar was a ruler of Babylon in the Chaldean Dynasty, reigning from 605 B.C. – 562 B.C. Often called "Nebuchadnezzar the Great," he is historically known for his grand building projects and the construction of the Hanging Gardens of Babylon, considered by many to be one of the Seven Wonders of the World.

Some of Nebuchadnezzar's illustrious reign is recorded in the Old Testament book of Daniel.

Daniel chapter 4 opens with an official proclamation made by Nebuchadnezzar which was circulated throughout his kingdom. As recorded in Daniel, Nebuchadnezzar writes:

> *King Nebuchadnezzar,*
>
> *To the peoples, nations and men of every language, who live in all the world:*
>
> *May you prosper greatly!*
>
> *It is my pleasure to tell you about the miraculous signs and wonders that the Most High God has performed for me.*
>
> *How great are his signs, how mighty his wonders!*
>
> *His kingdom is an eternal kingdom; his dominion endures from generation to generation.*[44]

In his letter, Nebuchadnezzar goes on to explain that life was good for him. He was relaxing in his palace, "content" and "prosperous," when he had a crazy dream about a huge tree that touched the sky and provided food and shelter for many. In his dream, a messenger from God ordered the tree to be cut down, its leaves stripped, and its fruit scattered.

Nebuchadnezzar approached all of his chief magicians and astrologers, but no one could interpret the dream.

Finally, exasperated by his efforts, Nebuchadnezzar approached Daniel, a young Hebrew boy he had taken captive during his siege of Jerusalem. Nebuchadnezzar did not acknowledge the God of the Hebrews, but Daniel had interpreted a previous dream for him, so he figured that he was a magician and had power from his gods.

God gave Daniel the ability to interpret king Nebuchadnezzar's dream, but before he explained the dream Daniel announced:

> *The Most High rules over the kingdoms of*
> *men and gives them to anyone he chooses.*[45]

What do you think Nebuchadnezzar thought of that?

Daniel was a "nobody" in Babylon. Actually, he was worse than a nobody; he was a captive Hebrew proclaiming that the God of the Hebrews, "The Most High," had ultimate authority over everyone – even Nebuchadnezzar.

Nebuchadnezzar believed that he was invincible because of his great power, wealth, and accomplishment. Given these factors, it's probably safe to assume that the people of Babylon believed Nebuchadnezzar to be invincible as well.

I wouldn't have wanted to be in the royal throne room the day Daniel told the king that his God rules over everything. Picture it:

Pandemonium breaks out. Everyone is running and screaming ancient Babylonian obscenities. The cup bearer's forehead furrows as he looks at Daniel in disbelief and exclaims, *"Oh, no he didn't . . . tell me he didn't just go there!"* One scribe whispers to another, *"That's not cool man – NOT COOL!"* The court jester mimics Daniel's voice repeating, *"The Most High rules, The Most High rules . . .,"* as he jumps around the room.

Wanting to know the point of this absurd Hebrew assertion, Nebuchadnezzar vehemently bangs his hand on the throne, demanding that Daniel continue with the interpretation…

The book of Daniel records the interpretation:

> This is what the dream means, Your Majesty, and what the Most High has declared will happen to you. You will be driven from human society, and you will live in the fields with the wild animals. You will eat grass like a cow, and you will be drenched with the dew of heaven. Seven periods of time will pass while you live this way, until you learn that the *Most High rules over the kingdoms of men and gives them to*

anyone he chooses. But the stump and the roots
were left in the ground. This means that you
will receive your kingdom back again when you
have learned that **heaven rules**.[46]

In boxing I think that's called the one-two punch!

Before Daniel even interpreted Nebuchadnezzar's dream,
he told the king and all his people that the dream was not the
problem, Nebuchadnezzar was.

Nebuchadnezzar and everyone else in Babylon believed
that Nebuchadnezzar was the sovereign authority over all
things. Nebuchadnezzar was the king; of course he was the
ultimate and final authority – right?

WRONG.

Nebuchadnezzar was a human ruler placed in leadership
by the ultimate and final authority over everything – GOD.

Having established the foundation for the discussion,
Daniel revealed the interpretation of the dream. As it turned
out, the dream contained the same message as Daniel's
forewarning:

> *The Most High rules over the kingdoms of men
> and gives them to anyone he chooses.*

The dream turned out to be a prophecy about
Nebuchadnezzar. God was sending Nebuchadnezzar a warning
– He was trying to tell him about *the real you* and exactly what
He wanted from him -- and everyone else for that matter.

Daniel predicted that "seven periods of time" (7 years) would pass in which Nebuchadnezzar would be expelled from his land and live like an animal – literally! (Next time you are bored, do a quick internet search on Nebuchadnezzar -- there are some pretty funny illustrations of him as half beast, half man).

This seems like a pretty harsh verdict. Nebuchadnezzar wasn't a bad king. In fact, he was one of the most prominent kings in Babylonian history. So why did God remove him from leadership and banish him to seven years with the farm animals?

The apostle Paul tells us the answer: "You can't ignore God and get away with it."[47]

Nebuchadnezzar had it all; wealth, fame, success and power. He was a respected king and a revered ruler. He and his people believed he was sovereign but he was not, and that is the point.

No matter who you are, what you think, what you say, or what you do – HEAVEN RULES. No matter how you look, what you wear, the car you drive, or the house you live in – HEAVEN RULES. No matter where you're from, where you're going, how you get there, or what you'll do when you arrive – HEAVEN RULES. No matter what you believe, or what you don't believe – HEAVEN ALWAYS RULES!

I'm not trying to make you feel small; I'm just passing along the all-important, fundamental, underlying truth that **you <u>are</u> small** when compared to the GLORY OF GOD.

Nebuchadnezzar had everything and lacked everything all at the same time. He was a BIG MAN, but so very small as well.

We are **small** too.

HEAVEN RULES

No one likes to be called small, especially not athletes, but that is exactly what you are.

After seven years on the farm, Nebuchadnezzar was restored to his kingdom, but not a moment before he had learned that heaven rules. In essence, Daniel told Nebuchadnezzar:

> You will receive your kingdom back again
>> when you have learned that ***heaven rules***.

In order to be restored to his kingdom, all Nebuchadnezzar had to do was learn one simple lesson--
HEAVEN RULES.

This is a hard lesson for anyone, let alone a king. Nebuchadnezzar spent seven years playing hop-scotch with his donkey friends. He had to become an animal to finally realize that God is not messing around; God is who God says that he is – THE KING.

When the seven years had passed, Nebuchadnezzar was restored to his earthly reign and all that accompanied it. He was back! The people's king. Ruler extraordinaire. But he was different. Nebuchadnezzar had learned that heaven rules and so he concludes his letter stating:

> I, Nebuchadnezzar, looked up to heaven. My sanity returned, and I praised and worshiped the Most High and honored the one who lives forever. His rule is everlasting, and his kingdom is eternal. All the people of the earth are nothing compared to him. He has the power to do as he pleases among the angels of heaven and with those who live on earth. No one can stop him or challenge him, saying, 'What do you mean by doing these things?'[48]
>
> Now I, Nebuchadnezzar, praise and exalt and glorify the King of heaven, because everything he does is right and all his ways are just. And those who walk in pride he is able to humble.[49]

This was the declaration of a changed man. There is no record of Nebuchadnezzar's involvement in organized sport, but we know he was a participant in the grand competition for glory.

Nebuchadnezzar spent most of his life competing for the sum of his own small significance. Granted, he was the star of the show. Nebuchadnezzar was king in the smallest, most insignificant, tiny, little pick-up game for his own glory, but God invited him to something more. God invited Nebuchadnezzar to become a part of, and compete in, the grandest, most important, coolest game of all games for God's glory.

God invites you to do the same.

COST OF ADMISSION

Like Nebuchadnezzar, God invites you to become a part of, and compete in, the grandest, most important, coolest game of all games, *the competition for God's glory.* As with any worthwhile sporting event there is a cost for admission. Decent seats for the MLB may cost $40, the NBA $60, the NFL may be upwards of $80-$100. Fans are willing to pay these prices because they want to be a part of the game; everyone wants to see what will happen as a result of the competition. The greater the competition, the more fans are willing to pay to see the game. The same is true for the participants.

Athletes love to compete. Most elite athletes are motivated by competition; the greater the level of competition, the more motivation there is to compete. Just as fans pay to watch the competition, there is a cost to compete as well.

No true athlete arrives at a competition without preparation. Every athlete pays a price to compete. Whether the price is as simple as the time it takes to practice the necessary skills for competition, or as extreme as the renunciation of friends, family and a life outside of sport, everyone pays a price.

God taught Nebuchadnezzar the cost of admission to the grand competition. It's pretty straightforward really – it's your life!

Simple, huh?

All God really wants is all of who you are; everything. He wants your time, talents, resources, and energy. He wants your mind, body, soul, and spirit. He wants all you've ever had, all you currently possess, and everything you might get one day. He wants it all; all of you for all of Him!

Your life is the cost of admission.

Jesus said, "Whoever tries to keep his life will lose it, and whoever loses his life will preserve it."[50]

That seems like a paradox but it's true. You were made for God; to know Him, to enjoy Him and to declare His significance. The more you try to keep your life for yourself the farther away you are from your life; the real you.

Jesus made a similar comment to his twelve best friends just before he sent them on a long journey. As his friends departed Jesus said, "If your first concern is to look after yourself, you'll never find yourself. But if you forget about yourself and look to me, you'll find both yourself and me."[51]

To participate in the grand competition for God's glory, you must be willing to sacrifice yourself. The crazy thing is that the more you sacrifice the more you gain. The same can be seen in sports.

The more you sacrifice to the game, the greater your potential return. When athletes sacrifice their time, resources, energy, and relationships for the game, the game rewards them. The reward might not always meet the expectation of the athlete, but a reward is inevitably rendered. The reward may be acceptance, popularity, personal achievement, or notoriety. If you are a professional athlete the reward may come in the form of increased financial remuneration. Regardless, sacrifice always yields a profit of some nature. The same is true with God.

God invites you to sacrifice your life so that you might be rewarded with the life he created you to have. That's not such a bad deal when you stop and think about it.

Sure, you forfeit the starring role in the small, small game that you have created for yourself, but you receive entrance into the greatest game of all time. No game past, present, or future will ever compare to the competition for glory, and God has selected YOU to participate.

THE WAIT IS OVER

I have been an athlete most of my life. I am passionate about my sport and I love to compete, but I hate to wait.

Think about it, sports provide a graduate education in patience. Most sporting events occur on the weekend. There is the occasional mid-week match, but the majority of sporting events happen at week's end.

Preparation for Saturday's game begins on Monday, and so does the wait. I don't mind practice but most athletes agree-- it's all about the game.

An athlete eats, drinks, sleeps, and trains in preparation for the game. As the week advances, preparation increases. As preparation increases so does anxiety. Great athletes do not fear the competition but they anxiously approach it because of the importance of the potential outcome.

Sport is all about winning and losing.

A popular women's soccer player once commented, "The person that said winning isn't everything, never won anything."[52] A popular American football coach often told his players, "Winning isn't everything, it's the only thing."[53]

Winning is very important to athletes.

Some athletes define their life by wins and losses. Winning can become an all-consuming force for some. One Major League Baseball owner commented, "Winning is the most important thing in my life, after breathing. Breathing first, winning next."[54]

Game day is a mixed bag of emotion. On the one hand you are excited to play, on the other hand you fear the unknown. That is a problem with sports -- you have to wait to see what happens.

Sometimes spectators are more impatient than the athletes. Many spectators feel a sense of ownership with the team. They may never compete, but they wait in eager expectation for the final result. Who will win and who will lose? This is the all-important question that everyone waits to resolve.

What if I told you the wait is over; you never need to wait to learn the outcome of a game again? Would that rob you of the joy of competition, or would it change the competition all together?

I think it would change the competition – for the good!

If you knew that every Saturday you would step on the field or court and win, how would that change your approach to the game? The competition would cease to be about me versus you, or my team versus your team, and it would become a competition to see how well you can play the game.

Nebuchadnezzar was a dominant force in his day. In sports terminology he was the undisputed heavyweight champion of his world. Although Nebuchadnezzar was unaccustomed to losing, he never met an opponent who could compete with him -- until he met God, that is.

God changed the goal posts on Nebuchadnezzar. God told Nebuchadnezzar that no matter who he was, what he had accomplished, or how great he might be, God is better – God always wins!

God wasn't necessarily bragging, He was just trying to help Nebuchadnezzar understand the real competition. The real competition is never about me versus you or my team versus your team. The real competition is always about my glory versus God's. Here's the thing, though – GOD ALWAYS WINS!

God told Nebuchadnezzar the same thing he tells us today; do not waste your time focused on the wrong objective. Paul wrote a letter explaining this phenomenon in which he said, "All created beings in heaven and on earth . . . will bow in worship before Jesus, and call out in praise that he is the Master of all . . ."[55]

Bottom line: God wins!

Whether you like it or not, "all created beings" will ultimately declare God as Master. In the meantime you can choose to participate in the grand competition for God's glory or you can choose to compete against God's glory, but either way you will compete and God will be declared glorious above all.

EVEL'S GLORY

A few months ago I saw a headline which read "Evel Submits to Good." That caught my attention so I started reading the article.

The story was about a man who had accomplished wonderful feats in his life. He is respected in his field and famous the world over. Wealth, women and wine accompanied this man's fame. He spent 68 years of his life believing he had it all. In fact, he once commented, "I've had a life better than any king, any president or any prince."[56]

Evel Knievel and king Nebuchadnezzar of Babylon believed the same thing – life is all about me. Of course, Evel Knievel and Nebuchadnezzar are not the only men in history to share that belief, but they are two public figures who now bear testimony to God's glory above all else.

Both men seemed to have everything; people believed they were invincible. Yet, as Nebuchadnezzar declared, "Those who walk in pride [God] is able to humble."[57] In the article Knievel said, "I know there's more to life than what I had." Just like you and me, Evel Knievel was made for something more. Despite his wealth, popularity and power, Knievel longed for God. Though he spent most of his life competing for his own glory, Evel Knievel finally came to compete for God's.

That seems like a paradox doesn't it – *Evel's glory*.

It seems like a paradox but it's true. Evel was made for God; to know him, to enjoy him, and to declare his significance.

Evel couldn't find his life until he lost it.

For 68 years it was all about Evel's glory, but finally it was about God's.

FOUR

Choice

FOUR

Choice

That Guy seems to show up everywhere.

You know the one. If you haven't met him personally, you've at least seen him around town. You can pick him out of a crowd with no effort at all. He's usually a large man, but he may be small. He's nobody and everybody all at once. You know—*That Guy.*

In the world of competitive sport, That Guy is always there. He (or sometimes she) is the individual at every game who seems to have received an unmitigated mandate to unrelentingly mock, make fun of, and verbally torment the opposing team. He takes pride in his arsenal of gratuitous one-line verbal jabs. He loves any opportunity to influence the game through hisself-assigned role as psycho fan. And he never misses a game.

Throughout my soccer playing career, I've come into contact with That Guy on a number of occasions and in a number of places, but none quite like Fresno. Fresno is a medium-size town in California, home of the Fresno Fuego soccer team. In Fresno, That Guy is a rather large man with a huge booming voice. He usually wears a Mexican sombrero and wields a vuvuzela. And he loves the Fresno Fuego. He sits dead center of the stadium rain or shine and comes to every game with an array of well-prepared insults. He has forever tainted my impression of the town.

While I've heard him shoot off any number of timely verbal darts over the years, none compare to his statement—or rather, question—"To who?!"

That's right. Of all the things this fan might say or do to ridicule the opposing team, the simple question *To who?* stands above the rest—it's That Guy's number one line!

To w-h-o?

Can you picture it?

The opposing team drives down the field, dissecting the Fuego with precision passing. A slightly overzealous player offers an errant pass in the final third of the field, and That Guy jumps to his feet, screaming *To who?*

It's the ultimate insult. With this simple question That Guy cuts to the core of the situation and ridicules the opposing team.

The opposing team takes a shot and misses high or wide . . . *To w-h-o?*

The opposing team throws the ball in, and Fresno intercepts it . . . *To w-h-o?*

At least five hundred times a game That Guy wants to know: *To w-h-o?*

It's "To Whom"

Before we move on, let's get one thing straight. Grammatically, it's *To Whom*, not *To Who!*

Every time we played the Fuego I was overwhelmingly compelled to correct That Guy's grammar, but I knew it would be an exercise in futility and just give him one more reason to mock me. That Guy doesn't care about proper grammar; he exists solely to torment the opposition.

I don't imagine that he intended anything more than mild provocation as he bellowed his interminable question. It was obnoxious and aggravating . . . but it wasn't altogether unwarranted.

I hate to admit it, but the more I have considered That Guy's question, the more I realize its potential validity. In fact, That Guy's question directly affects the real you.

The Real Question

As we discussed in Chapter One, the real you is the person that God created you to be, the person that exists for kabod—to display the weight and significance of who God is.

Yet for most of us the "weight and significance of who God is" is a fairly peripheral concept. It might serve as a fanciful fleeting thought, a nice thing to ponder on a Sunday afternoon, but it is not the resounding theme of our lives.

Enter That Guy.

Like it or not, he has hit the nail on the head. His question cannot be ignored.

To who?

It has very little to do with your passing accuracy or your ability to score a goal. The real question is more of a choice: *to who?*

It's the question that ultimately determines why you play the game.

The Race

While I was growing up, my dad was a fairly competitive long distance runner. Distance running was more than a hobby to him; running was his life (still is, actually). Though my dad was no Usain Bolt,[58] I was fairly certain that he was the greatest runner of all time.

I loved going to his races.

I remember the first race he ever ran. It started pretty early in the day, so my mom brought me to the finish line several hours after it had begun. Thousands of runners participated in the Sacramento marathon that cold December day, and as we arrived, the first runners were just about to finish. I remember the exhilaration I felt as I watched my dad run across the finish line.

I ran up to him and asked, "Did you win?"

He laughed as he shook his head no.

I couldn't believe it.

I asked a second time, *"Did you win?"*

He shook his head again.

How could this happen? Why didn't my dad win?

Frustrated and disillusioned, I sat in the very back seat of my parents' Ford Aerostar minivan as we drove home. After reviewing all possible scenarios, none of which seemed a sufficient answer, I yelled from the backseat, "Dad! Why didn't you win?"

Silence.

"Did you hear me?"

Silence.

Finally my mom said, "We're home!" and everyone piled out of the car—except me.

My dad is the king of calm. As everyone else rushed into the house, he circled around the back of the car, opened the hatchback door, and peeked over the seat where I lay prostrate.

"Everyone can't finish first every time," he said.

I pretended I wasn't listening.

He continued, "All the runners competed today, but winning the race looks different for everyone."

I don't remember the rest of that conversation, but I do remember the point: winning doesn't always look like you think it should.

Everyone Runs

The apostle Paul understood the race.

Paul was a Roman citizen, but he loved to travel. Following a visit to the ancient Greek city of Corinth, Paul wrote a letter to some friends he had made. His letter contained advice and thoughts on many Corinthian practices and utilized several different analogies to illustrate his point.

Paul wrote, "In a race everyone runs, but only one person gets the prize."[59]

Paul's Corinthian friends would have tracked with this comment at once because of their familiarity with the Olympic Games and other Pan-Hellenic games. These competitions all occurred on a four-year rotating cycle and included events such as chariot races, wrestling, various foot races, and *pankration*, a form of modern-day ultimate fighting. (Curiously, all ancient Pan-Hellenic games took place in the nude—all but chariot racing, of course.)

Throughout the ancient world it was widely understood that only Greek citizens were invited to compete in the games, but *all* Greeks were invited to compete. Paul was aware of this. He made reference to those who compete in a foot race, knowing this to be one of the most popular events.

Paul's comment on competition was the same as my dad's: *everyone can't finish first every time.* Paul and my dad understood what I like to call the Grand Competition of life—*the competition for glory.*

Whether you are a sportsman or not, you have been invited to compete in this Grand Competition. In fact, like it or not, you are competing.

As the apostle Paul says, everyone runs.

We all compete, but not everyone wins.

If everyone competes but not everyone wins, how do we compete to win?

Believe it or not, That Guy has the answer. Or rather, he has the question that leads to the answer.

That Guy Is God

On more than one occasion I have fantasized about meeting Fresno's That Guy in a dark alley and announcing "to whom" I'm about to lay the smack-down on. Since he outweighs me by at least a hundred pounds, it's probably not in my best interest to carry out that dream.

But his constant questioning and gratuitous one-liners are vexing, to say the least. After all, he's just a spectator. He's not the coach, he's not a player, he's not a referee, he doesn't even work at the stadium. He's just a guy sitting on the side critiquing the game.

But what if That Guy owned the other team— would that change the way you see him? Would you feel obligated to graciously accept his questioning? Maybe you would still be annoyed by his relentless banter, but might you find it easier to live with?

Or what if That Guy owned your team? What if the reason you were able to play the game was because he afforded you the opportunity? Sure, you are a valuable player -- you might even be the best player of all time. But without That Guy you would never have had a chance to play. Would that change your opinion?

For argument's sake, let's assume That Guy does own your team. In fact, he not only owns your team, he also owns the opposing team, the stadium, the parking lot, and the town; he owns it all.

What if That Guy is actually God?

A man named Asaph once wrote a poem about the authority of God. He said, "I [God] own the cattle on a thousand hills . . . all the world is mine and everything in it."[60]

The apostle Paul, who encountered God on his way to Damascus, learned that "there is only one God, the Father, who created everything."[61] Paul had spent years of his life fighting against and persecuting That Guy, who turned out to be God.

And if That Guy is actually God, it turns out that he is not just a guy sitting on the side critiquing the game. He actually created the game. He created all things for himself, to display the weight and significance of who he is.

But unlike Fresno's That Guy, who finds great pleasure in any frustration that may result from his verbal prodding, God does not delight in angering or vexing his creation; he simply desires to influence the game. More specifically, he wants to influence why you play the game—and that will affect *how* you play the game.

To Whom

If God is That Guy who attends every game, match, meet, or event, the one with the huge booming voice who sits center stage and continually bellows his interminable question, what is your response? Have you ever thought about that?

Remember, the real question has very little to do with your passing accuracy or your ability to score goals. The real question is more of a choice.

To whom do you play the game?

Let me put it a different way.

To whom will be the glory in your life?

Do you live, play, eat, sleep, work, run, drive, drink, laugh, cry, and sing for the glory of God or for the glory of you? Because, as we have been discussing, the real you is all about him.

You exist for him.

As American pastor and author Max Lucado wrote, "God does not exist to make a big deal out of us. We exist to make a big deal out of him."[62]

It's not about the money you can make, the rings on your fingers, the endorsement deals you sign, or the popularity you acquire. The fundamental question you must answer is *To whom will be the glory in your life?* No other question warrants quite as much attention from God, but the answer might not look as you would imagine.

Redefining Success

I have a friend who had a successful career as a sportsman. Recently he became a coach.

I called him to see how his first season as a university coach was going, and after some small talk about the weather in his new city and the whereabouts of some former teammates, I popped the question: "So tell me about your team?"

"Um . . . hmm . . . well . . ."

Okay, maybe that wasn't a good initial question.

"Well," I asked, "have you been winning or losing?"

"We've been forced to redefine success this season," he replied.

"What is that supposed to mean?"

"All I can say is that this season has taught me to see wins and losses in a whole new light."

The more I think about that conversation, the more I believe my friend has stumbled upon the secret of the Grand Competition.

Most competitive sportsmen or coaches will tell you that the reason they compete is to win.[63] Most define a win as a victory and a loss as a defeat. But maybe life's Grand Competition for significance involves a paradigm shift in our perspective. Maybe, like my friend, we need to redefine success.

Societal Success

Following that first marathon in Sacramento, my dad told me: *Winning doesn't always look like you think it should.*

For several years I thought that was the dumbest thing I'd ever heard (of course I didn't mention that to my dad). For much of my athletic career I maintained that winning and losing were universal values; no ambiguity, no room for debate.

A win is a victory.

A loss is a defeat.

Regardless of any postmodern notions of relativism, as people living in the technology age of the twenty-first century we generally migrate towards, and corporately affirm, clearly identifiable constructs. For example, if you attend the right university you are generally thought of as intelligent. If you drive the right car and live in the right house you are assumed to be successful. If you participate in the right committee and give money to the right charities you are considered socially responsible. Of course, there is a minority demographic that celebrates individualism, but it is clearly a minority.[64]

The same can be said of sportsmen.

As a sportsman, if you play for the right team in the right league and produce the right statistics, you are celebrated. When you win everyone seems for you, when you lose everyone seems against you.

The problem with this societal definition of success is that it may not line up with God's. In fact, our definition of success just might lead ultimately to failure.

The People's Choice

The Old Testament prophet Samuel tells the story of a mighty king named Saul.

Saul was thirty years old when Samuel anointed him as king over Israel. Samuel wrote that Saul was "the most handsome man in Israel—head and shoulders taller than anyone else in the land."[65] He came from a respected family with wealth, power, and prestige.

Saul would prove to be a strong military leader who won many battles for Israel. He seemed to have it all; subsequently, he was the people's choice.

At a certain point in Saul's forty-two-year reign, God gave

him a specific instruction to wage war against a people called the Amalekites. While Saul honored God's request, he did not do exactly what God had asked of him . . . and then he proceeded to construct a monument in his own honor. As a result, God told his prophet Samuel to anoint a new king over Israel. God sent him to see a man named Jesse, who had eight sons.

Samuel obeyed, but he was not happy about it. Several questions plagued him: What if he went to Jesse but couldn't find a king? How would the people react when they heard that their king had been replaced? And what if King Saul heard that Samuel was out looking for a new ruler—surely he would kill the prophet.

Arriving at Jesse's house, Samuel saw the oldest son, Eliab, and thought, "Surely this is the Lord's anointed!"[66] But God told Samuel, "Do not consider his appearance or his height, for I have rejected him. The Lord does not look at the things man looks at. Man looks at the outward appearance, but the Lord looks at the heart."[67]

Jesse would showcase seven of his sons one by one before Samuel found his king in David—the youngest, weakest, and most unlikely of the bunch.

Your Heart

Saul was the people's choice to be king.

David was God's choice.

Why?

Saul had it all. He had supermodel good looks, the best education, a prestigious heritage, and a proven track record as king.

David had nothing. He was a shepherd boy with no education, no prestige, and no experience.

Yet God chose David and rejected Saul because of God's view of success.

The prophet Samuel assumed that Eliab would be the perfect king because he fit the part. But God told Samuel: *Do not consider his appearance or his height, for I have rejected him.*

Do you see what just happened? God redefined success! The people wanted the strongest, most handsome, most prestigious man to be their ruler (naturally). God said: The Lord does not look at the things man looks at. Man looks at the outward appearance, but *the Lord looks at the heart*

Over 2500 years ago God told Samuel his criterion for success. It's not contingent on the money you can make, the rings on your fingers, the endorsement deals you sign, or the popularity you acquire. It's about the motivation of your heart, which leads to the purpose for your actions, which culminates in the things that you do.

Success begins with your heart, and that is why That Guy, who just might be God, is so insistent in his questioning: To whom?

God does not delight in your frustration or anger as a result of his persistent questioning; he simply wants to influence the game to ensure your success. Remember, God originally created the game of all games and intended for your utmost delight in participating. In the beginning there was no competition between God and man; everyone existed (competed) for the glory of God alone.

Unfortunately, Adam and Eve took it upon themselves to champion a new game. This game continues today as a very real alternative to God's game, and it is the one the culture will choose for you if you don't choose differently for yourself. As we've said already, this alternate game happens to be the smallest, most insignificant little pick-up game, but it is a very real option nonetheless.

The culture affirms your participation in this small, small game for your own glory. It celebrates the champions of this endeavor. In many cases you may not know in which game someone is competing; it isn't identified by tangible determinants, but by the heart of the competitor.

Regardless, the *choice* is yours.

Tenor's Choice

The story is told of a baker's son from Italy who loved to sing.

The boy was identified as a capable singer at an early age and tutored in the intricacies of the art of singing throughout his youth. At the same time, he received teacher's training and successfully completed a degree.

On graduating, the boy inquired of his father, "Shall I be a teacher or a singer?"

The baker replied, "If you try to sit on two chairs, you will fall between them. For life, you must choose one chair."

As the story goes, the boy made his choice and ultimately became one of the most famous tenors in the world—Luciano Pavarotti.

Reflecting on this all-important decision, Pavarotti would later comment, "I chose one. It took seven years of study and frustration before I made my first professional appearance. It took another seven to reach the Metropolitan Opera. And now I think whether it's laying bricks, writing a book—whatever we choose—we should give ourselves to it. Commitment, that's the key. Choose one chair."[68]

Choose one chair.

I realize it's not in vogue to choose. Keeping one's options open is the pattern of our world. Some think commitment is a four-letter word. After all, something better might come along, right?

Something Better

Something better has come along, but it has also existed eternally.

Originally, God created the grandest, most important, coolest game of all games, like the Super Bowl, Rugby World Cup Final, NBA Finals, and World Cup of soccer all rolled into one, but Adam and Eve decided God's game wasn't big enough and so they created their own.

The alternate game that Adam and Eve created does not affect God's game, but it does stand in direct competition. Now everyone has to make a choice.

Do you choose to compete in God's game for God's glory, or do you choose to compete in your game for your glory? You must choose or it will be chosen for you, and the choice will not be God.

Imagine that God is sitting on the sideline of your life. He is watching everything you do; he knows all of what you are and all of what he created you to be.

Maybe this is the first time you've noticed him sitting there. Or maybe you've noticed him in the past, but you've chosen to pretend that you didn't.

Do you hear what he is saying? He created you for success. He created you for victory. He created you for glory— *his own.*

God calls out . . . *To whom?*

You've heard the question. You know exactly what he wants to know

To whom will be the glory in your life? It's the question that awakens the real you. God will not force you to exist for his glory, but you sacrifice the real you when you don't.

The *real you* cannot exist for your own glory when you were created for God's. To do so would be antithetical. The *real you* is created for something much bigger, grander, larger, and more significant than the sum of all that you are on your own.

Of course, this may be a complete paradigm shift in your perspective on winning in life, but maybe winning doesn't look like you think it should. Maybe winning is even better than you thought. Maybe it involves much more than the things that you have, the things that you want, or the things that you can do. Maybe winning begins with your heart, and affects everything else as a result.

If That Guy turns out to be God who conspires for your ultimate success, the success he created the *real you* to know, and he asks you *To Whom?*--What will be your answer?

Which chair do you choose?

If you try to sit on two chairs, you will fall between them.

FIVE
One Box

FIVE
One Box

You're crazy. That's what a friend told me the other day.

This friend of mine is a successful media personality who has fought, scrapped and battled his way to mild celebrity status. This friend is not an athlete but he is involved in the grand competition as much as any athlete. Just like you, my friend is faced with a choice; to live for the glory of God or the glory of himself.

For the past few months my friend and I have been meeting in the front window seat of our local Starbucks by the falls. Every week he drinks a grande soy latte and I fluctuate between the tall Americano and peppermint tea. While our drinks fluctuate our conversation has been consistent – *the glory of God.*

Now several months into this ongoing dialogue my friend and I are at a standstill.

My friend believes that the significance of who he is

directly competes with the significance of who God is. He believes that God has created him for something more than the sum of his personal experience. He also believes that ultimately, God will be proclaimed as glorious above all else, but he wants to have his cake and eat it too.

My friend is happy to acknowledge all of the above but he doesn't want to feel restricted by dogmatic rules or "commands" as he calls them. Maybe you can relate?

I don't want to be bound by a set of legalistic parameters that dictate my life either. Some days I like the Americano, other days I prefer peppermint tea – that's my prerogative and I value it greatly. This said, the grand competition for glory doesn't actually interfere with your prerogative, and this is what my friend and I have been trying to unpack.

During our most recent meeting my friend asked, "If God wants all the glory, where do I fit in?"

We live in a celebrity culture in which everyone wants to be someone. I would be willing to bet that you are familiar with cyber social networking. Internet sites like MySpace and Facebook have exploded over the past decade. This is not a bad thing but it is very different than the culture of past societies. In past societies no one aspired to become a celebrity because celebrity was inherently assumed. A Columbia University anthropologist spoke about this phenomenon as he explained that "everyone is famous in a tribe."[69] In past societies everyone was a celebrity simply because they were a part of society, whereas only the elite qualified for celebrity status in more recent societies.

In our world, anybodies *and* nobodies can become somebody. In fact, nobodies can become celebrities without much effort at all – that's MySpace and Facebook in a nutshell; the average Joe becomes the celebrity of their own space.[70]

In our world everyone wants their space. This truism of our culture is at the root of my friend's question, *if God wants all the glory where do I fit in?*

It's a fair question.

God is not willing to share His glory with anyone or anything else, but He also created you to be unique, remember? In this, God is not opposed to your pursuit of your space; He only asks that the meditation, practice, and culmination of your space be to the ultimate promotion of His space.

My friend loves his celebrity status and all its accoutrements; popularity, respect, and influence. He also loves the glory of God. These two distinct loves seem to be contradictory, but maybe they are not?

YOUR SPACE CAN BE HIS SPACE

As we exist in the flesh, one of our greatest struggles will always be our underlying desire for our own benefit above other things. This is the nature of the Grand Competition initiated by

Adam's rebellion in the garden. Adam felt he could "orchestrate the game" better than God, and so he began to try.

We try too.

No one wants to admit they are selfish, but we are. As a people we are concerned about our stuff; my things, my stuff, my friends, my job, my family, my money, my space--more than we are concerned about others' stuff.

What if I told you that God can use your concern for you for Him?

What if your space can be His space at the same time?

The truth is, that was always God's plan; that your space would be His space. God's inceptive plan for His creation never encompassed a disunity of purpose, but provided for individualism as a facet of His design for His glory.

I think some of us have acquired a misperception of God. Some people view God as a tyrannical heaven-bound judge who exists to critique their life and impose stringent rules to be followed. They don't see God as a loving Creator who desperately wants communion with His creation. To these people, God is an impartial arbiter.

Other people have a misperception of God's opinion of them. God is not seen as a loving Father who is willing to go to great lengths to ensure his children's welfare. To these people, God is a meticulous referee, excited by the opportunity to accuse them of wrong.

In some arenas, the church has not helped us with a right perception of God. Actually, in certain circumstances, the church has served to negatively (and incorrectly) portray God. It is no wonder that some of us have a misperception of God. This is a regrettable reality, but it certainly does not negate the true God who is both Creator and Judge, yet deeply cares for the welfare of his creation with the white-hot passion of a father for his child. This God who created all things great and small is so concerned about the intimate details of your life that in light of our Adam-initiated rebellion he did not sit on the sideline and observe the game; he left the stands and became a player in the form of his son Jesus Christ.

The greatest information that I have ever come across is that God thinks so highly of me that he would leave his space (in all its grandeur) and enter my space (in all its humility) to reopen the door to his game. Through Jesus, God is inviting YOU to become all of who He created YOU to be *for Him*. He longs for the *real you* to emerge.

God created YOU to be YOU.

God wants your space to become his space; he doesn't want or need you to relinquish your space in order for that to happen.

FLIGHT

I have a no-nonsense friend who works in construction. He always tells me that I like "philosophy" to much. At first I was confused by this comment, but I think he means that I like to philosophize.

My friend often says, "Gimme it straight up."

I could philosophize about that expression but I'll give it to you straight up: *God wants your story to count for His-story.*

At the moment my coffee friend and I are at a standstill because he is struggling to understand how his story can be used for God's, and what parts of his story are usable. Rather than continuing to unsuccessfully philosophize around the same point, I recently changed the conversation.

My friend and I have spent two months talking about the glory of God and his unique role in what I call the Grand Competition. Like I said, my friend understands, and even agrees with all that we have been discussing, but he's failing to connect the dots.

Maybe you feel the same?

A few years ago I was flying to Los Angeles and I sat next to a business executive in a chic suit. As I seem to travel frequently, I've formulated certain stereotypes about people I meet en route. Of course, these are stereotypes and only my opinion based on observation, but I generally find that people dressed to impress on an airplane are significantly less talkative than the more modestly dressed group. My admirably dressed seatmate on the way to Los Angeles was an exception to my rule.

Shortly after the flight departed Cleveland Hopkins International airport the conversation began. I now refer to it as "the conversation" because it was one of those crazy long events you can only generalize about in retrospect.

The conversation twisted and turned around numerous topics over a four-hour time period, but one topic stood out: faith.

CHURCHED UP

I'll be honest, I love talking with people on airplanes as it provides a predetermined period of time and somewhat of a captive audience. I don't usually have an agenda, but I often try to take people's spiritual temperature to see where they stand. If the person seems interested in talking about spiritual things I'm happy to do that; if not, I don't push it. My businessman friend was more than willing to speak about spiritual things, though I suppose it was a natural conversation given the fact that Easter was later that week.

I asked him, "Are you heading to church on Sunday?"

"Oh yeah," he responded.

His response seemed fairly enthusiastic so I prodded a bit further.

"That's cool, what church do you attend?"

"Hmmm….well….I don't know the name because I don't go too often, but I love getting all churched up when I have the opportunity."

I had to think about that for a second.

*I LOVE GETTING ALL **CHURCHED UP**.*

What does that mean? I don't think it was a bad answer but it caught me off guard.

***CHURCHED UP**.*

It's like church or God or Jesus are some sort of psychoactive substance like caffeine; a substance that when injected acts as a stimulant drug which produces a euphoric high for a time and then slowly dissipates.

Don't get me wrong, church can be pretty exciting stuff, as are God and Jesus, but ***churched up*** left me wondering.

WORLDVIEW

The more I chatted with the businessman in the chic suit on his way to Los Angeles, the more I learned about him. As it pertains to spiritual things, I do believe that man had a desire to know God and honor him with his life. In fact, I think that he knew quite a lot about God and Jesus and church. The problem wasn't this man's knowledge of God, it was his perspective.

We began talking about perspective in the last chapter as we discussed a potential need to redefine success which would ultimately necessitate a paradigm shift for some of us.

The English language can be tricky because many words have multiple meanings. For example, if someone were to ask you to discuss your perspective on a particular topic you would probably respond with a statement of *opinion* about that topic. This would be an acceptable response as perspective does suggest opinion. Yet, perspective also suggests a *paradigm*, a concept which finds its origins in the Greek language and addresses a more general frame of reference or way of viewing a certain situation, thing, or topic.

A popular author and leadership guru explains a paradigm as "the way we see the world – not in terms of our visual sight, but in terms of perceiving, understanding, and interpreting." [71]

Paradigm: a matter of perceiving, understanding, and interpreting the world.

You can think of paradigm like a pair of sunglasses. Not only do you view the world through the glasses, but the way you view the world is shaded by the glasses that you wear. Some people wear rose-colored glasses. Some wear polarized. Others wear UV protectant. Each of those glasses has different lenses which directly impact the things that you see and the way that you see them.

So, your perspective isn't limited to your *opinion* on a particular topic, it actually includes the reason you are of the opinion you hold and that's called *worldview.*

Because everyone has a worldview and everyone tends towards some level of narcissism, most people tend to believe their worldview is right. This is almost never a conscious belief, but as our leadership guru friend comments, "Each of us tends to think we see things as they are, that we are objective. But this is not the case. We see the world, not as it is, but as we are – or, as we are conditioned to see it. When we open our mouths to describe what we see, we in effect describe ourselves, our perceptions, our paradigms. When other people disagree with us, we immediately think something is wrong with them."[72]

I was reminded of this last night as I hosted a coloring contest with my two nieces (ages 2 and 4). Prior to the contest we discussed the rules; you could only use the specified colors and all coloring must be complete within the allotted ten minute time period.

After about forty five seconds the four year old screamed, "I'm done, Uncle!"

We all held up our pictures to compare. The two year old had only managed to chew on the magenta crayon, so her picture was uncolored. The four year old had in fact completed her picture, but an outsider might conclude she's color-blind and suffers from Tourette's syndrome, and I had carefully colored the hair and beard of my character but hadn't done much more.

The four-year-old looked at all the pictures and then furrowed her brow as she said, "I'm a much better color-er than you are uncle. . . I win!"

We see the world, not as it is, but as we are . . .

If this is true then my businessman friend on the airplane, the barista that pulled the shots for my morning Americano, the car technician that just charged me way too much to fix my car, and pretty much everyone else in the world need to consider why we are who we are.

ENCULTURATION

I'm not sure about you, but I quite like myself. I find that most competitive athletes have some level of self-like.

This is a good thing.

Many people struggle with self-dislike. I'm not a trained psychologist so I shouldn't comment on the psychological reasons for self-like or dislike, but I am an observer of culture who has noticed a pattern.

Have you noticed that a culture is shaped by its people but it also shapes its people?

Let me give you an example.

Have you ever heard of Starbucks? I'm guessing you have. Prior to the mid-1980's Starbucks was a small Seattle-based coffeehouse that very few people outside of Seattle would have heard of. Over the past twenty years Starbucks has become the largest coffeehouse company in the world.[73] In 1987 Starbucks was nothing more than 11 coffee shops in the Pacific Northwest of the United States. Twenty years later Starbucks is a multinational company with over 15,000 stores worldwide.

Do you think Starbucks has influenced your life?

It seems crazy but companies like Starbucks which are being shaped by average people in a culture are also shaping the culture in which they exist.

Who had ever heard of a Frappuccino before Starbucks? What about tall, grande or venti drink sizes? Starbucks set out to create their own coffee culture, which has resulted in a global coffee phenomenon that has changed the culture around them.

This cultural phenomenon is not unique to Starbucks. What about companies like Macintosh? Gadgets such as the iPod, iPhone and iTouch are now shaping the culture in which we live. I was recently on a crowded train during Washington D.C. rush hour. You could hear a pin drop as nearly everyone on the train was transfixed in an iPod coma. At one point an elderly woman boarded the train and tried to engage her seatmate in conversation. The seatmate, who had her iPod pumping, didn't notice the woman speaking and exited the train at the next stop.

People shape culture.

Culture shapes people.

This is critical information as it relates to your worldview because the way you view everything, including yourself, is directly affected by the culture in which you live. One author calls this "enculturation;" the process by which culture influences a person.[74]

BOXES

Unless you live alone in an underground nuclear bomb shelter in Outer Mongolia you have been influenced by culture. This is not all bad as there are some very positive aspects to culture. Yet, culture is never a good guide in things pertaining to the *real you*. Granted, one can learn a great deal about the *real you* in terms of what *not* to do from certain cultural icons, but generally the real you will struggle to emerge if culture is your primary instructor.

This was the topic of my most recent Starbucks-by-the-Falls discussion. I told my friend what I told you about him earlier, he wants to "have his cake and eat it too." I'm not sure that I fully comprehend that expression, but when I use it I'm referring to my friend's desire to love, follow, and honor God, but also to choose the times and places he will do so.

It's no mystery as to why my friend feels like this; culture affirms this belief; not necessarily in relation to God, but certainly as a general rule of thumb.

Have you ever heard this expression, "What happens in Vegas stays in Vegas?"

I've got nothing against Vegas. In fact, I'm thrilled that 350-pound Elvis still performs there nightly, but expressions like this convey the culturally held belief that life happens in a box--multiple boxes to be exact.

As proud as some people might be, thinking our generation had something to do with the life in a box phenomenon, this belief is actually not an invention of modern culture. Almost 2,000 years ago the apostle Paul spent a significant amount of time in a city called Corinth. The Corinthians, as they were called, also believed that life happens in a box. Corinth was widely known as a "party town." Before some of the people of Corinth began following God, they were among some of the most blatant carousers and loved to indulge in most everything. It is suggested that Corinthians followed the creed "eat, drink and be merry for tomorrow you die."

Paul once told some people in Corinth, "Everything is permissible for me – but not everything is beneficial."[75] Paul was a devoted follower of God who knew how to have a good time. He wasn't trying to condemn every social activity in Corinth, he really just wanted the Corinthian people to understand the real you and their "fit" in a world created by and for God.

Even though many Corinthian people devoted their life to God, they continually struggled to fully maximize their potential to use their life for God. Corinthian culture dictated Corinthian practice. Here's an example.

As a culture the Corinthians believed that the body and the spirit are separate. This fostered a belief that you could do what you wanted with your body without affecting your spirit.

Corinthian God-followers took this cultural belief system and inadvertently integrated it with their new faith. It seems silly 2,000 years later, but many Corinthian God-followers went to church two times per week. The first time they went to have sex with the prostitutes that hung out at the church, the second time they went to corporately worship God. This was perfectly acceptable behavior for a devout Corinthian follower of God.

Sex on Saturday.

Worship on Sunday.

Pretty standard, really.

Whether you are a God-follower or not, this probably doesn't seem like acceptable behavior to most people today. In our culture it's largely taboo to frequent prostitutes, especially for those who claim to be religiously inclined.

How could that behavior be acceptable? Didn't those people have any moral standards? Yes, of course they had moral standards. In many ways the moral standards of first century Corinthians were much higher than those we generally maintain today, but seemingly unacceptable practices became acceptable because of the Corinthian worldview – life in a box. Because Corinthians believed the body and spirit were separate (i.e., they existed in different boxes) they could go crazy with their body at the temple on Saturday and worship God freely, without guilt, on Sunday.

Paul didn't tell these new followers of God that they had to stop that behavior, but he warned them that it might not be the most beneficial if they wanted to leverage their life for God – *Everything is permissible for me – but not everything is beneficial.*

We face a similar predicament today. Ok, the church is not generally advocating the solicitation of temple prostitutes, but many aspects of our daily life is shaped by a culture that continues to suggest life in a box; not one box, but many.

ONE BOX NOT MANY

We live in a society in which everyone wants their own space. Call it what you will, I call this life in a box; not one box, but many. There may be any number of boxes in which we live. Most have a box for family. A separate box may exist for friends. Some have a work box. Others maintain a recreation box. It makes sense that there would be a God box if you are inclined towards God.

Pondering the businessman in the chic suit on his way to Los Angeles it struck me -- *"churched up,"* I get it, that's the God box! Wanting to clarify this sudden revelation, I asked him to explain.

"You know, I get my dose of God and then I attack the rest of life . . . I get churched up," he said with a grin.

Just then I heard the "bing-bong" noise that signifies arrival and freedom to exit the plane. Everyone began rushing around collecting their stuff. The lady in front of us hit me on the head as she tried to pull her bag out of overhead compartment. The guy in back kept pushing us forward saying he was late for his connecting flight. The conversation was over.

As I've thought about the businessman in the chic suit on his way to Los Angeles, I've often thought about God in a box. The more I think about God in a box the more I think that God probably isn't so particular about being in a box as long as his God Box encompasses every other box. Yet, I suppose if it were the case that God's box encompassed every other box, there wouldn't really be multiple boxes but many parts of one box.

Maybe that's the point?

YOUR FIT IN GOD'S BOX

A few hours ago my friend and I met in the front window seat of our local Starbucks by the falls. He drank a grande soy latte and I had a peppermint tea. We lamented the realities of Cleveland weather, laughed about a friend who got his head stuck in his door (long story), and then continued with the glory of God discussion we began two months ago.

"I think I've figured it out, Aaron!"

"What's that," I asked?

"I've figured out where I fit with the glory of God."

"What a breakthrough!" I thought to myself. I'm still daily working out my "fit," but I was thrilled for my friend.

He went on to tell me all about his childhood dream of becoming an actor and his age 16 discovery that he couldn't act to save his life (for the sake of confidentiality I won't reveal the circumstances that lead to his discovery; you should ask him if you ever meet him!). He shared about how his dream to become an actor had changed into a dream to be on television in some capacity and how he had worked his entire life to see that dream become reality.

My friend made it.

He is on television 5 mornings per week.

He loves what he does.

My friend became a God follower during college. He was always a good guy but he had little knowledge (or interest) in Jesus, and God's plan for his life. My friend had a plan he was fairly confident in. When he asked Jesus to become his savior and gave his life to God his freshman year of college, he quickly gained an insatiable desire to know and honor God. This desire pulsed through every aspect of the new God box in his life. The problem, as he describes it now, was that any number of other boxes competed with his God box.

At one point my friend remembers thinking, "I want to serve God but I'm in television." My friend's perspective of God affected his life in God.

At that point we arrived where we had begun several months prior. My friend said that he'd been wrestling with God because he doesn't want to give up his career in television but he wants to use his life for God's glory.

I could relate.

For many years I felt the same way about my athletic career. I wanted to serve God and glorify him with my life -- but I was an athlete. I remember thinking, "What does God have to do with soccer?"

One day I stood on a field in the middle-of-nowhere, Africa as I watched God use soccer to impact many lives. I remember thinking of a Jewish girl called Esther who was raised by her uncle in the ancient city of Babylon. At a certain point Esther had become the queen of Babylon and she was faced with a difficult decision. As she deliberated about the decision, Esther failed to realize that God had allowed her to become the queen. God wanted to use Esther's story for His-story.[76]

That afternoon on the soccer field in the middle-of-nowhere, Africa I realized that God wanted to use my story for His-story. I didn't have to change my story; I needed to yield my story to God.

I think my friend has discovered the same thing.

We laughed about how small we are in comparison to God and then concluded that maybe culture isn't so far off after all?

Culture says that we have absolute freedom to do and be what we want, so does God. The only difference is that God wants you to use your space for the promotion of His space; one box that encompasses every other box.

Walking out of Starbucks I passed a book of quotes. I opened to the first page and read this: "We must not cease from exploration and the end of all our exploring will be to arrive where we began and to know the place for the first time."[77]

I think that's where my friend and I have landed this day.

Grande soy latte, tall Americano or peppermint tea -- call me crazy but I think you can choose what you will as long as you use it for the glory of God.

SIX
Soli Deo Gloria

SIX
Soli Deo Gloria

I recently realized that my childhood bedroom is a memorial to sports in the 1980s. Now, you need to understand that I haven't lived with my parents in well over a decade, but they have perfectly preserved my former bedroom. Soccer ball wallpaper, Ruud Gullit poster, and my prized eighth-grade flag football MVP trophy—they've kept it all!

On my most recent visit home I was rummaging through some of the old junk in my room and I found two soccer balls I bought at the 1994 World Cup of Soccer in the United States.

I loved those two balls.

I actually remember the exact day I bought them. The U.S. was playing Brazil in the second round, and a friend had given me a ticket to the match (that ticket is still in my room as well). As a kid growing up in America, I don't think I had ever experienced true soccer culture until that day. Thousands of Brazilian fans had converged on the Bay Area of California. Pregame parties had been rocking for hours before my friends and I arrived at the stadium. By the time we arrived, the famous Brazilian samba was in full force and people were so excited that some were physically hanging from the light posts along the streets in front of the stadium.

Wanting to be a part of the action, my friends and I decided to buy a ball. Well, my friends decided that I should buy a ball. Caught up in the emotion of the event, I bought two balls: one was the official World Cup match ball, the other a replica. I stowed the official match ball in my backpack and we immediately began dribbling through the frenzied crowd with the other.

Over a decade later these two originally identical balls look very different. Following that World Cup match in 1994, I remember carefully placing the official ball on a display shelf in my room—where it still sits, of course. It still looks like new. Of course it's flat and outdated, but there's not so much as a grass stain on its surface.

The replica, on the other hand, is old and tattered. I never had a storage spot for it because it was always in use. You can hardly tell the two balls were once identical.

The Same but Different

Do you ever wonder what inanimate objects might say if they could talk? I get it, it won't happen . . . but *what if* my two World Cup soccer balls could talk . . . what do you think they would say?

Both balls were created the same. I suppose they have slightly different properties, making one more expensive than the other, but they were made for the same purpose—to be kicked, passed, trapped, and generally put to use. One ball is now beat down and tattered while the other looks as new as the day I bought it.

They are the same but different.

I wonder which ball got the better deal?

I think the same thing about people sometimes. Everyone is created the same, but different. We all have traits that make us unique, yet we have the same purpose—to glorify God in and through our lives.

As we've been discussing, the glory of God has always been God's purpose for each of us. He gives everyone certain tools to use for his glory; the Bible calls these tools gifts. A guy called Peter once instructed, "God has given you gifts . . . manage them well. . . ."[78]

No one is without a gift. The difference is found in how we manage, or use, the gifts we have been given.

Amadeus

Growing up, I loved the 1984 movie classic *Amadeus*. The story is fiction, loosely based on the lives of two composers from the Classical era, Wolfgang Amadeus Mozart and Antonio Salieri. Both musicians lived in Vienna, Austria during the latter half of the eighteenth century.

The movie opens with Salieri as an old man sitting in a lunatic asylum because he had attempted suicide. He is visited by a young priest who tries to convince Salieri to confess to the rumored murder of Mozart. Salieri remains silent until the priest says, "All men are equal in God's eyes." Salieri responds, "Are they?" and launches into his story about the relationship between himself and Mozart. As it turns out, Salieri didn't murder Mozart . . . but he wished he had, as he was tormented by Mozart's musical genius most of his life.

Most intriguing to me is Salieri's transition from a God-fearing man who credited his talent and career to God, to a man who devoted his life to oppose God and God's plan for Mozart. At one point in the movie Mozart has just spontaneously "improved" on a piece of music Salieri had toiled to create. Recognizing Mozart's musical genius, the enraged Salieri yells at a crucifix:

> "From now on we are enemies, you and I. Because you choose for your instrument a boastful, lustful, smutty, infantile boy and give me for reward only the ability to recognize the incarnation. Because you are unjust, unfair, unkind, I will block you, I swear it. I will hinder and harm your creature on earth as far as I am able."

Have you ever felt like Salieri?

Salieri was a gifted and celebrated musician in his own right, but he was so jealous of Mozart he could never embrace his own talent. Salieri and Mozart were created for the same purpose and given certain gifts to fulfill that purpose. The resounding difference between their lives was the way they managed the gifts they'd received.

Rather than trying to honor God with what he had, Salieri's jealousy drove him to spend his life thwarting the successful use of another man's gifts. In essence, Salieri set his gifts on a shelf while Mozart was out using his.

In watching *Amadeus* I'm quick to judge Salieri's obvious misuse of his potential. But before we ridicule Salieri, consider Jesus' advice: "It's easy to see a smudge on your neighbor's face and be oblivious to the ugly sneer on your own."[79]

Maybe we are more like Salieri than we think?

Salieri was caught in the briars on the very small side of the competition for glory. When you get right down to it, Salieri couldn't get past the pursuit of his own game. Antonio Salieri loved Antonio Salieri's glory.

Saved

The smudge on Salieri's face seems fairly obvious, but what about the ugly sneer on my own? Salieri is not alone in his pursuit of his own glory. This may shock and disappoint you, but you should know that I have a preoccupation with my own glory as well. I know; it's a problem when you aspire to write books about God, and God's glory above all things . . . but the truth is that we all pursue our own glory in one way or another. That doesn't excuse my personal pursuit, but it does comfort me knowing we are all in this together.

The apostle Paul once taught on the universal pursuit of personal glory. He wrote, "There is no difference, for all have sinned and fall short of the glory of God."[80]

There is no difference, for *all* have sinned.

The great news is that God knows the condition of our heart and he's okay with it. Well, he's not exactly okay with our sin or the fact that we continually seek to promote ourselves above him, thus missing the mark of perfection he created us to know. But what he is okay with is the solution he provided, and a right response to the provision he desires us to have.

The Bible explains that just over two thousand years ago God looked upon humankind and could no longer tolerate the way our sin had put us at cross-purposes with him. So God offered the only provision that could reconcile us to him once and for all: he gave his son, Jesus Christ, as propitiation for man's sin.

Propitiation is a big Bible word, but it's not actually so complex; it just means an "offering that turns away wrath." That was what God did in allowing Jesus, who was both perfectly God and perfectly man, to live without sin and then die an unjust death on a cross so that the wrath of God might be satisfied and man's unity with God restored.

One of the greatest mysteries of the Christian faith to me is propitiation; God no longer holds me responsible for my sin because Jesus gave his life as an offering to cover my sin and reconcile me to God.

God is not angry with me; in fact, because of Jesus' propitiation, God now invites me to be *for him*.

Have you ever really thought about that?

Paul told a different group that their universal pursuit of personal glory alienated and left them "enemies" of God.[81] Yet God made a way; he offered propitiation so that we might be his friends instead.

If you've hung around church circles you're likely to have heard the term saved in reference to God's propitiation for sin and your acceptance of his sacrifice.

When I was in high school I wasn't so much of a church guy. But I did enjoy attending the Christian group on campus because all the attractive ladies seemed to congregate there. One day, following a particularly meaningful Christian club meeting the night before (meaningful in regard to the high attendance of lovely ladies, of course), a girl approached me and said, "I heard you are saved! That's great, can you pray for so-and- so?"

Not wanting to blow my cover as a church guy, thereby potentially blowing my cover as trusted church guy friend to many lovely church girls, I quickly gathered my wits and gave what I thought was the appropriate answer. "Of course, I'm definitely saved! Being saved is so cool, isn't it? Tell so-and-so that since I'm saved I'll definitely pray."

There was an awkward silence for a good half minute, and then the girl said, "O . . . kaay . . ." and slowly walked away.

I was pretty proud of my answer. I was also fairly certain that I had maintained my church guy cover. It wasn't until a few years later that I realized what an idiot I was.

I realize now that I probably wasn't "saved" at all back in high school, but the word stayed with me. During my freshman year in college I met a guy who loved to play table tennis as much as I do. As it turned out, he happened to be a very committed, wonderful follower of God.

One night after he had beaten me (again), something compelled me to ask Brian, "Are you *saved?*"

And he said, "Yes, I am. Why do you ask?"

That night Brian explained the craziest, most wonderful information I had ever heard. Brian said that because God loved me so much, he wanted me to exist for him. But because of my sin, God, who is perfect and without sin, cannot be united with me unless I, like him, am perfect and without sin.

Up until that point I had known that God was perfect and I was not, but I figured that I could appease Him as long as I tried to be a good person.

That night I heard a message that changed my life—that because of my sin and rebellion against God, God allowed his

Son to live a perfect life and suffer an unjust death on a cross as a propitiation for all the ways in which *I* sin and fall short of God's glory, so that *I* could be saved from a life separated from God and his purpose for me.

I remember that day clearly because it was the first time I had ever heard and understood that anyone who accepts Jesus' sacrifice is saved from their sin and no longer separated from God.

As we walked home that night Brian asked, "So are you saved?"

"I think I am . . . now," I responded.

Saved *to* Something

It seems I may not have been the only person who is in the dark about being saved. I speak to people all around the world who have no idea what that means. I usually tell these people not to worry since I was a church guy for twenty years and I didn't know what it meant either.

These days I speak and write about life with God and his glory. I don't often use the word saved when speaking about becoming a follower of God, but I'm beginning to think that I should.

Being saved seems to have garnered negative connotations within today's society. We love our space, so we don't want to be saved from it. In fact, it seems that when people are saved, they are saved from something they don't know if they *want* to be saved *from*—themselves. While I do believe that there is much to be saved from, I'd rather focus on what we are saved *to*.

A guy called Timothy was the apostle Paul's right-hand man. Towards the end of Paul's life he wrote Timothy a letter in which he urged him to "take hold of the life that is truly life."[82]

Jesus said that he is the life that is truly life. He said, "My purpose is to give life in all its fullness."[83] Another translation says it like this, "I came so they can have real and eternal life, more and better life than they ever dreamed of."[84]

God offered Jesus as a propitiation for our sin so that we might be saved to the life that is truly life; a better life than we ever dreamed of.

Saved *for* Something

I'm willing to bet that if you are a person who reads section titles you have already figured out what's coming next. (If you're not a person who reads section titles, then shame on you; we authors toil and sweat to create those insightful little two- or three-word headings. Okay, just kidding. I write the first thing that comes into my head and then quickly move on.) But seriously, look at this section heading: Saved for Something. Surely you can guess what it is you've been saved for?

It seems a bit redundant at this point, but I'm going to say it anyway: You've been saved for God's glory.

You see, as much as God's act of propitiation is about us, it's also about him. In fact, everything God does is about God and his glory; subsequently, everything we do should be about God's glory as well.

I recently read a good book called *Searching for God Knows What*. The first chapter was all about formulas people use to relate to God and how "formulas presuppose God is more a computer or a circus monkey than an intelligent Being."[85] I agreed. But then I thought, maybe sometimes God appreciates formulas. I wish no offense to the book's wonderful Christian author, Donald Miller, but as I think about what we have been saved *for*, namely the glory of God, it occurs to me that a formula might be exactly what we need.

Priests, Princes, and Paupers

Several hundred years ago, 491 years to be exact, a man named Martin Luther nailed a document containing 95 statements of disagreement with the Roman Catholic church (the "95 Theses") to the Wittenberg Castle Church door in Germany. Luther and his colleagues were protesting many of the practices of the Church; it was a protest that would ultimately lead to the formation of "Protest-antism."

I'm not equipped or qualified to provide an in-depth lesson in church history, but the Protestant Reformation bears consideration.

Prior to Luther's posting his protest on the church door, participating in the glory of God was a lot more complex for the average Joe. The Bible was not written in a language common people could read, nor was it encouraged that those outside the priesthood read it anyway. As a result, only a select group of people had access to the knowledge of the Bible, and the churchwas shaped by this select group.

Along came Luther, who said, among other things, that all people should have the opportunity to read God's word for themselves. Part of the problem in those days was a hierarchy the church had established in which the priests ranked as most important. It seems the church believed that all people were created by God and for God, but not equally. It's sort of like a football team in which the quarterback is the most important player because he's the only one who knows the plays.

God had extended the invitation for all people to compete for his glory, but no one but the priests knew about it. As long as the priests had the play book, they had the power. In effect, Martin Luther reclaimed the power for the people. As a result the people did not become more powerful than the priests, but they realized that priests, princes, and paupers were all equally made for the glory of God.

A guy called Peter, whose name in Greek literally translates "Rock," was fundamental in the initial establishment of the Christian faith. Peter wrote a letter to the God-followers of his day. In the letter he addressed his audience as a "royal priesthood"[86] of people belonging to God. The title *royal priesthood* would have taken some people by surprise, as the majority of the letter's recipients were average, everyday people—not priests.

Let's put this in context. It's as if you were to receive a letter that addressed you as King or President So-and-So. As much as you might like the sound of it, you'd have to admit that the title wasn't accurate. But what if it was?

That's what Peter was saying.

That's what Martin Luther said as well.

Priesthood of All Believers

God had a plan from the very beginning to use you for his glory. He's always known what you would look like. What you'd be interested in. What you'd love. What you'd hate. What you'd dream about. What you'd get excited about. And everything else that makes you you.

God's plan did not begin when Peter wrote his letter, or when Martin Luther nailed the 95 statements on the church door 1,500 years later. The Word of God says, "He [God] chose us in him before the foundation of the world . . . in love he predestined us to adoption as sons through Jesus Christ to himself."[87]

Prior to Martin Luther a formula existed in his culture that looked something like this:

God + Priest + You = Potential for God's glory

I suppose that wasn't such a bad formula, as most priests are godly, decent men who have accepted a vocational responsibility to point people towards God. But Luther wanted everyone to know there's a better way. And so a new formula emerged following Martin Luther's courageous act of rebellion and protest against the church hierarchy:

God + You = Potential for God's glory That's the priesthood of all believers.

God + YOU = Potential for God's glory

It's really that simple.

If you are connected to God through his Son Jesus Christ, you are of the royal priesthood! *God + You* is a formula that releases your potential in God. It's the formula that releases the real you.

Tokyo Disney

A few years back I was flying from Bangkok, Thailand to Tokyo, Japan. Prior to landing, the flight attendant handed me an arrival card to fill out. It's all fairly straightforward stuff unless you don't know where you are staying in the particular country you are visiting.

The friend with whom I was traveling didn't know either. I searched through the in-flight magazine for the name of a hotel in Tokyo—my standard practice in this scenario—but I couldn't find anything. Limited by our knowledge of Japan, we finally decided that Tokyo Disney would be a safe bet.

My friend Jon went through customs first. He walked up, greeted the small man in the window, handed him his arrival card, and promptly made his way through the gate.

It worked! I thought.

I approached the same man confidently, handed him my arrival card, and waited. The man looked at me for five or ten seconds, then looked at my arrival card. Looked at me. Looked at my arrival card. This went on for several minutes. The longer I stood there, the worse the heinous crime I had committed in identifying a false hotel became in my mind.

He called for backup. Two other agents began the ritual of gazing at the arrival card. Finally they all started laughing and shaking their heads in agreement. The first man pointed at me and declared in broken English, "Yur feemoush shinger!"

I had *no* clue what he was saying. If I stood there very still, I thought, he might just let me pass.

Another agent exclaimed, "You feemous shinger!"

"Oh! No, no, I'm not a *singer,*" I shouted.

They huddled in bewilderment, then retorted, "Yur feemoush danscher!"

"What? . . . No. No. I'm not a dancer, either!"

The agents were obviously growing impatient with my hidden identity. . . .

"Yur not feemoush shinger?

"No," I said.

"Yur not feemoush danshcer?"

"I'm sorry, I'm not," I responded.

"Then why you stay at Tokyo Disney?!"

Identity

Despite their obvious disappointment, the customs agents did let me into Tokyo that day. I won't even try to guess why they thought I was a singer or a dancer. But I suppose they weren't as concerned about my occupation as they were about my identity.

It's a pretty important question really: Who are you?

Growing up, I was always The Soccer Guy. A friend of mine told me that she was The Homecoming Queen. It's funny how activities or events can define us in our culture.

I suppose I've never minded being known as the soccer guy, and my friend said she liked the title homecoming queen. But is that it? Do those titles really define our person? Are they our identity? And if they are, should they be?

The more I think about it, the more it seems that there should be some line of separation between identity and activity.

Activities like soccer, accounting, or skydiving are just that—activities—but an identity is the essence of who you are as a person.

So . . . who are you?

Following that run-in with the Japanese customs agents I thought a lot about that question. Anyone who stands within a ten-yard radius of me at church can confirm that I'm not a singer. I'm certainly not a dancer, though I'm not afraid to bust-a-move when called upon. Soccer Guy had always been my alias, but soccer might not last forever. I started having a mini-crisis. And that's when I heard about Martin Luther.

Basically, Luther wanted everyone to know they are the same but different. Priests, princes, and paupers are all the same because the essence of who they are is defined by God, not by the things they do or by what other people say of them.

Remember what Paul said, "He [God] chose us in him before the foundation of the world . . . in love he predestined us to adoption as sons through Jesus Christ to himself."[88] This is either a very bold fairytale passed down for thousands of years or it is God's truth about who we are, his sons and daughters through Jesus Christ.

Shortly after I left Japan I decided that Martin Luther was right about my identity—it is the same as everyone else's identity through Jesus. And along with this revelation I realized that our sameness allows for differences.

Same Purpose, Different Activities

I was seated in the back corner of an open-air conference room/cafeteria in Haiti. Four fans mounted on the ceiling provided my only tangible hope for comfort as the man in the front explained something about physical education in Haiti's native language, Creole.

In a few minutes I was going to address a group of roughly fifty physical education teachers. My talk was entitled "God Loves P.E."

While I cannot communicate in the native Haitian language, I hoped to convey the same biblical truth that I had shared with a group of used car salespeople in California the week before and with some high school science teachers the week before that: God loves the activities his people are involved in when they are used for God's glory.

One of my favorite, yet most frustrating verses in the Bible says, "So whether you eat or drink or whatever you do, do it all for the glory of God."[89]

I love that verse because it speaks about God's love for the things I love. When I read this verse I'm struck by its simplicity. "Whether you eat or drink . . . do it all for the glory of God." I think to myself, huh, I'm pretty good at eating, I'm sure I can do that for God's glory. And drinking, I'm not sure exactly what that means, but I'm fairly certain that I can drink for God's glory too.

The thing about eating and drinking is that they are only one part of a bigger picture. Eating and drinking are activities that God says he loves when they are used for his glory, but "whatever you do," that's when it starts to get tricky.

Whatever you do can be an activity, but when you start to add up all the activities in your life they cease to be activities and they become a *lifestyle*.

I suppose that is the point.

Priests, princes, and paupers were created by God for God in every aspect of life. They are the same in purpose but different in activity. Priests don't participate in the same activities as princes, who differ from paupers. Princes might like polo, paupers prefer boxing. Priests like poetry, princes like parties. It's all the same, though.

Same God.

Same purpose.

But different activities.

Sacred Versus Secular

When communicating cross-linguistically you never can tell what's lost in translation, but my new Haitian friends and I all had a good time. At one point during my talk, a young guy sitting in the front of the room said, "My pastor says sports are too secular to use for God. What do you think?"

I could see how his pastor might think that. Sport can be a pretty dark world full of corruption, greed, cheating, and pride, for starters. I'm sure God looks at the sports world and shakes his head in sadness for what it is at times. I'm also positive that was never God's intention.

Paul said, "For everything comes from him; everything exists by his power and is intended for his glory."[90] The last time I checked, everything meant all things, and that includes sports. Of course, we live in a world that has been tainted by the entrance of sin, but inceptively everything was created by God for God. Because of sin, everything now competes for or against God's glory.

Jesus once told a group of religious people, "He who is not with me is against me, and he who does not gather with me, scatters."[91] That seems a little black or white for my liking, but the point is clear. In all things, you are either for God or against Him.

In 1942 an Englishman named George Orwell wrote an essay entitled Pacifism and War in which he commented, "If you hamper the war effort of one side you automatically help that of the other. Nor is there any real way of remaining outside such a war as the present one. In practice, 'he that is not with me is against me'. The idea that you can somehow remain aloof from and superior to the struggle . . . is a bourgeois illusion."[92]

Orwell understood Jesus' point: "You're either with me or against me."

That makes me think of my friend Glen, who I mentioned in Chapter One. You remember the table tennis competition and Glen's departing words: "The war continues." If given a choice, most of us would refrain from war, but this is our spiritual reality. I have heard it said that in life there is not a war side and a not-war side—life is war!

This said, my young Haitian friend's question about his pastor's concern with the secularity of sport is completely valid and important. When it comes right down to it, the real question is what can or cannot be used for the glory of God? If sport is too secular, what about music? I can think of some pretty secular songs/ singers these days. What about videography? Or drama? Or business? Or preaching, for that matter? I don't want to point fingers, but it seems to me that there are some horribly secular preachers on TV. If sport is too secular for God, maybe all of the above are too?

Jesus once ransacked the temple in Jerusalem, shouting and turning over all the tables and chairs. After he had concluded his tirade he quoted the Old Testament prophets Isaiah and Jeremiah, who said, "My house will be called a house of prayer for all nations. But you have made it a den of robbers."[93] It seems that secularism is a problem everywhere.

Maybe the real problem isn't so much the things we use to glorify God, but rather the people who use the things.

In high school I did not live my life for God, but I pretended like I did. Whatever my reasoning, it's safe to conclude that anything I did was secular. If I played soccer it was a secular activity. If I watched TV it was a secular activity. If I brushed my teeth it was a secular activity. Why? Because I, Aaron Tredway, was secular.

Isn't that what Martin Luther and Peter were saying in calling God followers a "royal priesthood?" Peter followed that statement with this one: "Once you were not a people, but now you are the people of God; once you had not received mercy, but now you have received mercy."[94] *You're either with me or against me; sacred or secular.*

I could be wrong, but I think the Bible says that *things* are not sacred or secular, *people* are. Didn't that verse say, "So whether *it* eats or drinks or whatever it does, *it* should do it all for the glory of God?" No, that would be silly! Paul was a real person speaking to other real people about their real lives. He said, "So whether you eat or drink or whatever *you* do, do it all for the glory of God."[95]

SDG

Earlier we looked at the Hollywood version of the life of Mozart. Salieri, as portrayed in the film *Amadeus*, doesn't think his rival is using his God-given talent appropriately. Mozart replies, "I am a composer and was born to be a *Kapellmeister*. I neither can nor ought to bury the talent for composition with which God in his goodness has so richly endowed me."[96]

The apostle Paul wrote, "So here's what I want you to do, God helping you: Take your everyday, ordinary life—your sleeping, eating, going-to-work, and walking-around life—and place it before God as an offering."[97]

Mozart may have acknowledged God as the source of his genius, but another famous composer, Johann Sebastian Bach, went farther—Bach leveraged his life as an offering for God's glory.

Bach preceded Mozart by just a few years and was born in Austria's neighboring country, Germany. While Bach was never the focus of a major Hollywood film, he was one of the most gifted and famous composers of all time, and his music is still widely known and revered today.

I'm not sure what church Bach attended. I don't know much about his theological disposition. The one thing that is certain is that Bach sought to glorify God with his entire life. On the bottom right corner of every score Bach produced he would write three letters—SDG.

SDG is an acronym for *Soli Deo Gloria*, a Latin phrase meaning "glory to God alone." During the time of Martin Luther and the Protestant Reformation, this phrase emerged as one "The Five Solas," the foundation on which most Protestant faith is built. In addition, there was *Sola Scriptura, Solo Christo, Sola Gratia* and *Sola Fide*, but *Soli Deo Gloria* encapsulates the other four.

By Bach's day The Five Solas would have been widely known. I could imagine that older ladies would probably knit Five Sola macramé to hang in a frame on the family room wall or cross-stitch it on a pillow cover.

Glory to God Alone.

In writing SDG at the bottom of every score, Bach was proclaiming that his work, the talent it took to create it, and ultimately his life were *only for God's glory*. Bach chose to take his everyday, ordinary life—his sleeping, eating, going-to-work, and walking-around life—and proclaim *Soli Deo Gloria*.

Participants

This makes me think of my two World Cup soccer balls.

Both balls were created for the same purpose—to be kicked, passed, trapped, and generally utilized. One ball is now beat down and tattered while the other looks as new as the day I bought it.

What do you think those two soccer balls would say about their lives?

One ball routinely offered itself for the purpose for which it was made. It might be said of the replica ball that it never had as much potential as the official match ball; it wasn't quite as gifted. Yet the replica was used and the match ball was not.

I bet if the match ball could talk it would tell you it missed the point of existence.

God went out of his way to create everything for his glory; soccer balls, musicians, sixteenth-century reformers, and you and me. The Bible is pretty clear that God also went out of his way to save us. Not in a weird, televangelist, send me eighty dollars and you can be healed type way, but in and through the wonderful, awe-inspiring, very real sacrifice of his only begotten Son on the cross as a propitiation for our sin. In Christ we are saved from our own small existence and invited to bring all we've got to God's game—for *His glory.*

One of my favorite modern-day Christian authors, Os Guinness, says, "There is no higher/lower, sacred/secular, perfect/permitted, contemplative/active or first class/second class... the business person, the teacher, the factory worker, and the television anchor— can do God's work (or fail to do it) just as much as the minister and the missionary."[98]

I love that God gives us a choice.

I hope you don't choose to sit on the shelf. I think the match ball would admit it's no way to spend your life.

SEVEN

Vapor

SEVEN
Vapor

When I was a kid, my friends and I thought Adidas was an acronym for *All Day I Dream About Soccer*. We, of course, would not have thought the [S] to represent another activity like some older kids on our block. Regardless, Adidas seems to be somewhat synonymous with soccer.

Last summer Adidas ran a series of commercials called the *One Game* campaign. I'm not sure how many commercials the campaign produced, but I saw at least four over the summer months. I generally loathe commercials, but these were interesting.

The *One Game* campaign was built around the global influence of soccer and the World Cup held in Germany. The point, as far as I could tell, was to illustrate soccer as something more than a game, and then link the Adidas brand to this positive force in the world. I liked every commercial I saw, but one really impacted me. Maybe you saw it? The commercial

was all about how Senegal's qualification for the World Cup
brought peace to a nation involved in many years of civil
war. Apparently, Senegalese rival forces had been at war in
Senegal for over 20 years, but upon qualification for the World
Cup, representative leadership from each group gathered and
collectively decided to stop the war, so as not to hinder their
team's potential for success in the tournament. That's pretty
amazing if you ask me.

Another particularly impactful One Game commercial
scrolled short statements across a black screen. It said something
like, "*ONE GAME* . . . closes shops; closes the schools; closes
a city; stops a war; fuels a nation; breaks the boarders; builds
a hero; crushes a dream; answers a prayer; and changes the
world." The commercial concluded in stating:

ONE GAME CHANGES EVERYTHING.

Now, I'm a soccer guy so you could understand how
exciting Adidas' *One Game* assertions might be to me. Outside
of an occasional tear in particularly moving moments, like when
Rocky Balboa defeats that insane Russian guy in Rocky III, or
when I was 17 and found out Santa Claus isn't real (kidding,
I was 15)--outside of that, I'm not really a "cry-er." That said,
when I first saw the Adidas Senegal commercial I couldn't
contain myself.

One game *changes* EVERYTHING.

What a crazy, confounding, miraculous truth.

SPORT IS NOT LIFE

Sport is NOT life, but it is pretty close.

All around the world, sport serves as a glimmer of light in what can be a grey and dreary existence for many people. It's sad but true. If you're not a sports person you probably think the above idea to be a total farce or, at the very least, a laughable oddity. Yet, regrettably, I do speak the truth. Like it or not, sport offers hope to the hopeless. It's actually a biblical idea, I think.

The apostle Paul said, "God chose the foolish things of the world to shame the wise."[99]

If you ask me, sport qualifies as one of those "foolish things" Paul was talking about. Take baseball for example; 1 guy is trying to hurl a leather rock past another guy holding a stick while all his buddies stand around scratching themselves and waiting for the leather rock to come towards them. How about tennis? Tennis involves 2 or 4 people who attempt to volley a bouncing eraser over a net; first side to hit the eraser short, wide, or long looses. What, sport--foolish? Never. Foolish or not, sport is a global language. Forget about English--sport is far more widely spoken.

The former President of South African once said, "Sport has the power to unite people in a way little else can. It breaks down racial barriers, it laughs in the face of all kinds of discrimination. Sport speaks to people in a language they can understand."[100]

I didn't grow up thinking, "I should play soccer because it unites people, breaks down racial barriers and laughs in the face of discrimination." I played because it was fun. It is fun. I like competition and camaraderie and physical exertion and winning. I like yelling and jumping and kicking and sweating.

I like sport, it's not life but it's pretty close.

SIDON

If sport is the "global language," then soccer is English.

I'm not trying to boast or promote soccer just because I happen to like it, but it's true, soccer is the world's game. Those of us who live in the United States don't always have the opportunity to witness this first-hand, but I have seen it on several occasions.

A few years ago I was invited to play on a soccer team that traveled through the Middle East for three weeks. I didn't know what to expect as I had never visited that region of the world. The experience turned out to be unbelievable. Amongst other things, our team drove along the road to Damascus, the same road on which the apostle Paul encountered Jesus, and participated in a cultural festival with nomadic Lebanese mountain-dwelling people called the Druze.

The Druze are a fascinating people with a wonderfully rich heritage of faith and community. Interestingly, the Druze hold the belief that the Messiah has not yet come but will do so in the form of a man. Subsequently, every Druze male wears a type of the pants made popular by the artist formerly known as M.C. Hammer. It's fascinating really, and quite a sight when worn as part of a soccer uniform with cleats, shin guards, and Nike headbands (I'll leave that to you to visualize).

Whether we were with the Druze people in the mountains of Lebanon, the Jordanian police in the southern city of Aqaba, or the Hezbollah in the ancient biblical city Tyre, soccer was our point of connection.

While I loved touring the Middle East, I remember having to depart on the trip early. One of my teammates, a Swedish guy named Thomas and I, departed Beirut on the same flight to Europe. We left the team riding camels in Petra, Jordan and traveled to a city called Sidon in Lebanon the night before our flight. Thomas had a friend in Sidon who agreed to house us for the night and then drop us at the Beirut airport the next morning.

That tour was several years ago so I probably wouldn't remember the 8-hour random encounter with Thomas' friends in Sidon, but there was something unique and wonderful about them.

Thomas' friends, Gary and Bonnie, had not been married long when they felt led to use their lives for God's glory in Sidon. I think they had been in Sidon for about a year when I met them; both had a purpose and passion I quickly admired.

As they showed Thomas and me around the city they now
called home, a city steeped in Christian history yet overcome
by civil war and a militant sect of Islam, they beamed with
excitement over what God was beginning to do in this once
great city.

Later that night we all sat at an open air table by the
Adriatic sea and chatted about Gary and Bonnie's work in Sidon
over some really great coffee and Lebanese pastries. I don't
remember what Gary did but I remember Bonnie was a delivery
room nurse for unwed Palestinian mothers. I think I remember
that because Bonnie had such compassion and empathy for the
women she cared for. I remember thinking about the danger
Gary and Bonnie encountered because of their decision to live
and work in Sidon, a largely Hezbollah area, and the respect I
had for their work.

We chatted by the sea until about 2 in the morning, slept
for a few hours, and Gary dropped us off at the airport at 6 am.

KHARTOUM

A few years later I was violently awakened by a cock-a-
doodling rooster in Mozambique, I think we may have eaten
the same rooster later in the week, but I try not to think about
that part.

I remember the day that I was awakened by the cock-a-
doodling rooster because it was the same day I wrote a letter to

my friends and family explaining why I hadn't returned from Khartoum, Sudan. Now, I hadn't been to Khartoum at that point, but in preparation to go to Khartoum the leadership of our soccer team felt it would be wise to have every player write a letter to friends and family and leave them in a lock-box in the Johannesburg airport.

I remember that day vividly because I had never seen so many grown men huddled together crying about something that hadn't actually happened.

At the time our team went to Sudan, Khartoum was widely known as a base for several anti-American terrorist groups. Politically it was strongly recommended that our team refrain from visiting Khartoum. In meeting with the U.S. consulate in Washington D.C., we were told the trip would be "permitted but not promoted." As a result, we were told that the U.S. government would accept no responsibility for our safety if the team was to visit Khartoum. We decided to go anyway.

That was the day we all wrote the letters.

I remember sitting beneath a huge African baobab tree as I pondered the words for my letter. How do you start a letter explaining something like that?

"Dear everyone, I'm dead . . . "

It's seems crazy to even write something like that now, from the perspective of several years later.

I sat under the African baobab tree for hours and wrote nothing. I had a pen. I had paper. I had a clipboard to write on, but I couldn't do it. I wanted to be brave and bold and say something like, "To live is Christ, to die is gain . . . I've gone the way of gain!" I couldn't do it.

I thought about my family, my niece that was about to be born, and all the things I really love about life. I thought about my goals and aspirations and all the things I still wanted to experience. I would start to write the letter and then, each time, I would crumple it up and throw it behind the baobab tree.

How do you explain a decision you feel is right but that ultimately terminates life?

Eventually we all produced our letters. We all committed our lives to God and prayed for His protection. We all boarded the plane in Johannesburg, connected through Nairobi, and landed in Khartoum. We all played in the game against the national team, traveled in a bus with no air conditioning across the Sahara desert for 9 hours (both ways), and witnessed as God did miracles through the willingness of a handful of normal people who wrote a letter and went to Sudan.

THE VOICE

I returned home from Khartoum ready to go anywhere, do anything and tell anyone who would listen that God is real, He's faithful and He wants to use our lives for His glory!

It was fall and the air was brisk in Cleveland. The day after I came home I had planned to play in an indoor soccer game and then join some friends for dinner and a movie, or something like that. As I drove to the indoor soccer complex near my house, I thought about how much I like the fall and how creative God must be to think up so many different plants and trees and leaves and colors.

I don't often listen to the Christian talk radio station in Cleveland, but it was on that day. In fact, I was about to change the station when I heard the voice. It was familiar, but I couldn't place it. I started listening to the discussion being broadcast from Moody Bible Institute in Chicago. The guy being interviewed was obviously distraught as he spoke about his wife who had passed away. I could swear I knew the voice but I couldn't place it.

The guy talked about his wife's heart for God and her love for people. He never mentioned her name. He never mentioned his name. Though I came into the broadcast late I gathered that he and his wife were Christian missionaries who were fairly young, who had been serving in a hostile environment. I listened intently trying to place the voice and then he said it:

My wife loved the women she served and the babies she delivered.

I couldn't believe what I was hearing. I turned the car around immediately and drove straight home frantically, wondering if this woman who died and her husband who spoke on the radio were the same couple I had spent 8 hours with in Lebanon a few years prior.

I ran into the house, opened my laptop and tried to remember their names. I didn't need to. The headline confirmed my fear; Bonnie was dead.

LIFE IS SHORT

Throughout the weeks directly following the news of Bonnie's death, I existed in a semi-comatose state. I thought a lot about life, purpose, and the ways of God. I don't know that I ever came to any great revelations during those weeks, but life became much more important to me.

A few years back my friend started an organization called Vapor Sports Ministries. Over the past few years, Vapor has focused on bringing the hope of Jesus to people living in the second largest slum in Africa through sports facility development and youth leagues. The work is amazing but so is the name.

My friend Micah who founded the organization always signs his e-mails, "Life is short." Below that he quotes a Jewish poet: "As for man, his days are like grass, he flourishes like a flower of the field; the wind blows over it and it is gone."[101]

That's what I realized following Bonnie's death; *life is short.*

Young people don't usually spend much time pondering the brevity of life, but maybe we should? Though a subconscious thought, I'm generally of the belief that I'm invincible, life is unlimited, and opportunity abounds. Most young people I meet feel the same way. We aren't talking about it, but I think we believe it. If actions speak for beliefs then it's not hard to see.

Remember our daredevil friend, Evel Knievel? I was running on the treadmill at the gym the other day and I saw on CNN that he has died. I'm not trying to depress you, but you probably realize that death is inevitable. It's like someone once said, "The only sure things in life are death and taxes." Honestly, I don't really fancy either.

WORTHLESS IDOLS

The Bible talks about a guy called Jonah who tried to hide from God. You may remember Jonah's story from your childhood days? Jonah was the Jewish prophet whom God told to go to Nineveh to warn them of impending destruction. The Bible says:

> One day long ago, GOD's Word came to Jonah, Amittai's son: "Up on your feet and on your way to the big city of Nineveh! Preach to them. They're in a bad way and I can't ignore it any longer." But Jonah got up and went the other direction to Tarshish, running away from GOD. He went down to

the port of Joppa and found a ship headed for Tarshish. He
paid the fare and went on board, joining those going to
Tarshish—as far away from GOD as he could get.[102]

I think it was the former heavyweight champion Joe
Louis who first said, "You can run but you can't hide!"

God had a job for Jonah, but he took off in the other
direction. Once he was on the boat to Tarshish, God caused
a huge storm to swell on the ocean and threaten the lives of
all on board. Everyone on the boat began freaking out and
frantically debating about whose god was mad. In a bold move,
they all drew sticks and determined it was Jonah (I still don't
really get that part but it happened). The men questioned
Jonah; he confessed he was running from God, they threw him
overboard, and a whale swallowed him whole.

Maybe you remember what happened next?

I suppose it's pretty obvious. Jonah didn't have many
options, so he prayed. Amongst other profound things Jonah
prayed about while hanging out in the whale's stomach, Jonah
confessed, "Those who cling to worthless idols forfeit the grace
that could be theirs."[103]

Jonah never really makes it clear what he meant by
worthless idols, but this Hebrew expression literally translates
to mean "empty nothings." Jonah was saying that in running

away from God's plan for his life, he was running towards desolation, vanity, or – *empty nothings.*

It's easy to judge Jonah as an elusive heathen scoundrel on the run from God but he was a prophet. Sure, Jonah ran from God when he was asked to speak to the Ninevites but it's no small fact that he was chosen by God to speak on God's behalf. A prophet is a proclaimer, one who speaks for God, in the name of God, and who carries God's message to the people. Though Jonah ran from God he couldn't escape his true calling. We're not so different from Jonah.

Jonah wasn't running from God so much as he was running from the *real you.* I've realized that I'm inclined to do the same. That inclination is part of the unfortunate fabric of reality you and I inherited from Adam and Eve's rebellion. I don't believe that Jonah was opposed to God's best for his life, or that he desired to actively resist the man God created him to be; Jonah's problem was that he thought he knew best. If you're really honest with yourself you will probably admit to the same. I know that's true for me. I love to speak about how God is in control, how God loves me, and how God has a plan for my greatest good, but then, inevitably, I so often find myself metaphorically sailing on a boat towards Tarshish and I wonder what went wrong?

Can you relate?

If you are an athlete the sports world is your Nineveh. You may not have noticed the formal invitation to take God into the sports world but it's there.

Matthew was a tax collector who Jesus called a friend. Having spent several years traveling, speaking and hanging out with Jesus, Matthew wrote a wonderful account about his experience with Jesus and some of the stuff Jesus had taught him. Matthew recounts one of Jesus' most famous teachings spoken publicly to his twelve closest friends and a large crowd of on lookers on a mountain near Capernaum. On that mountain Jesus told His followers that they are the "light of the world."[104] He also warned His followers not to hide their light but to "allow your light to shine" for everyone to see.

In no uncertain terms, Jesus was telling all who would choose to follow Him that they are prophets. Now, not all God-followers are prophets in the Old Testament whimsically chatting with God in the cool of the day type sense, but rather, those empowered as proclaimers, who speak for God, in the name of God, and who carry God's message to others – *prophets.*

I don't know if Jonah liked being a prophet or not but that is what he was. That is what we are as well.

Paraphrased into modern language, Jesus literally told those who would follow Him, "You're here to be light...God is not a secret to be kept...If I make you light-bearers, you don't think I'm going to hide you under a bucket, do you? I'm putting you on a light stand"[105] so others can see my light.

YOU'RE HERE TO BE A **LIGHT**.

Whether you are in a classroom, on a field, with a patient, in an office or preaching on a Sunday morning, the *real you* exists to showcase God. Jonah might tell you that the pursuit of anything less adds up to a whole lot of nothing – *empty nothings*, I suppose.

THE LIGHT

The other day my friend was telling me about a trip he took to Afghanistan. We spoke about some of the more serious implications of his trip but I must confess that I was much more intrigued by his watch.

You need to understand that ever since I met my friend Jon he has worn the same watch, or at least that's what I thought. It's not like Jon's watch is anything special really. Actually, Jon told me the other day that you can buy it for $9.99 at almost any Walmart. It's nothing special, but Jon loves it. Every time the watch breaks, the wrist band snaps, or the battery expires, Jon buys a new one – the same one he's always worn.

The reason Jon's watch intrigues me so much is because of its light. Please understand this; it's a really cheap watch. I tease Jon all the time, but he doesn't care. He always says, "I know how to work this watch – I'm keeping it!" And so, Jon was recently in Afghanistan sleeping in a garage with no electricity. Having only just arrived that afternoon, Jon was not yet acquainted with his surroundings when he went to sleep. This is not a problem for those of us who manage to make it through the night without having to go to the bathroom, but for babies and aging adults apparently this is a problem.

Jon explained to me that sometime around 3:30 in the morning he realized he couldn't wait until morning; he had to go. Fumbling to find his way in the extreme black of the garage with no electricity, Jon remembered his watch. At this point in the story Jon holds up the wrist to which his watch is eternally fastened in an almost heroic gesture of pride and gratitude. He proceeded to explain how his seemingly insignificant little watch from Walmart has a light which just so happened to be bright enough to illuminate the entire garage, thus ultimately lighting his path to relief. The watch seems pretty average but apparently the light makes the difference. If you ask me, that's probably not so far from an accurate description of you and me: it's the **light** that makes the difference.

Jesus said, "I am the **light** of the world. If you follow me, you won't be stumbling through the darkness, because you will have the light that leads to life."[106]

I'm not sure about you, but that makes me think that life is a lot more about the light than it is about watch bands, batteries, and all the other stuff I love to think about.

INCARNATION

While I only met Bonnie for a few hours one balmy summer night in Sidon, her life and death impacted me. More than anything, Bonnie's life caused me to take stock of my own. You see, if we are like grass or a flower of the field passing with the wind, every day counts, right?

When I was five I remember attending my first soccer practice. I remember getting out of the car and walking towards the field. My dad attached some funny plastic things to my leg, pulled bright yellow socks over them all the way up to my thigh, and said, "Have fun!" It only took me a few minutes to realize I was made to play soccer. Years later I returned to the same field. By that point I felt I had accomplished many of my dreams as an athlete. It was the off-season and some of my teammates were visiting me at my parent's house. We decided to play a quick game of soccer before proceeding with the other events of the day.

I remember running down the side of the field warming up with my friend Justin. When we reached the end of the field Justin stopped for a second, looked at me and said, "Aaron, I was born to do these things." I wasn't so sure what he meant but I nodded.

Justin pointed at the ball near his right foot and said, "I was born to have this ball at my feet, to travel around, and to entertain people with my soccer ability." I started to catch on, shook my head in agreement and said, "So was I!"

I spent most of my youth believing soccer was life. Bonnie's death caused me to reexamine that belief. The more I thought about it the more I started to believe that sport is pretty insignificant in the grand scheme of life. After all, it's just a game, right?

It's true; sports in and of themselves are just a bunch of insignificant games--but what if the light of the world, which is life, was to be involved? What if Jesus was a part of the game?

I remember a song by Joan Osbourne that posed a similar question. Osbourne's song asked, "What if God was one of us?" The song posed lots of questions about what God might be like if He was down on earth like you and me, an average, everyday type person. I remember wanting to send Joan Osbourne a copy of the New Testament, or the gospel of John. Even if she just read John's opening statement, "In the beginning was the Word, and the Word was with God, and the Word was God…The Word became flesh and made his dwelling among us,"[107] she would probably find an answer to her unremitting question.

The Bible is pretty clear about God's interest in our lives. Though fully capable of directing the action from afar, Jesus entered our world, lived like us (though devoid of sin), and left a model for us to follow. Jesus, *the light*, got involved with the darkness and wants us to do the same.

NINEVEH EVERYWHERE

What if God came to you and told you to go to the worst, most vile, corrupt, hedonistic place on earth? Do you think you would go? That was Jonah's dilemma. God was not asking Jonah to do anything He wasn't willing to do Himself, but Jonah chose another route. Funny, in the end that route led him to Nineveh anyway; he just took the long way around the barn, so to speak.

Ever since I first heard about Jonah I've wanted to be different. Not necessarily different from everyone else, but certainly different from Jonah. Jonah had seen the glory of God--in fact, Jonah often spoke about the glory of God in his role as a prophet, but he still ran. The tricky thing about society today is that we don't need to look very far to find Nineveh. God went to Jonah and told him to leave his comfort zone and go to Nineveh. As best I can tell, the difference today is that most of us already live there.

A popular Christian author noticed something similar. He writes, "The problem with Christians [today] is not that they aren't where they should be but that they aren't what they should be where they are."[108]

We Christians are always looking for ways we can serve God or events we can participate in that will allow us to communicate our faith. Don't get me wrong, I believe that God wants that from us. Even more, I believe God wants that *for us*, but maybe there's something more? Maybe life isn't supposed to be so much about events and activities, but more about a lifestyle?

In Jonah's day he had to travel a great distance to find Nineveh, a city filled with people in desperate need of *the light*. Today we don't have to go anywhere; those in need of the light are all around us. I'm not trying to discredit the work of brave and wonderful Christian people like Gary and Bonnie who left friends and family and home and comfort to take the light to Sidon, but if everyone went to Sidon, who would illuminate the rest of the dark in the world?

One of the most beautiful things about the Christian faith is the community formed by those who love and follow Christ. The biblical title for this community is the *body of believers*. The apostle Paul mentioned the body of believers several times, and he often compared it to a human body; one body with many parts. Paul wrote, "Just as each of us has one body with many members, and these members do not all have the same function, so in Christ we who are many form one body, and each member belongs to all the others."[109] Paul concluded his analogy about the body by stating, "Since we find ourselves fashioned into all these excellently formed and marvelously functioning parts in Christ's body, let's just go ahead and be what we were made to be, without enviously or pridefully comparing ourselves with each other, or trying to be something we aren't."[110]

LET'S GO AHEAD AND BE WHAT WE WERE MADE TO BE.

I think that is a grand idea. Don't you want to be what you were made to be instead of pretending to be something that you're not? Maybe your problem is that you don't know what you're supposed to be? There's a ton of choices, right? I always wanted to be a doctor, but then I saw a show about people who wear cool uniforms, drive as fast as they want wherever they want, and carry a gun to protect society. After that I wanted to be a cop. There's any number of great things to do. Helpful things. Necessary things. Things that count for something and make a difference. Yet, at the core of our being, we were made in the image of God to reflect the image of God. Everything else is secondary.

Jesus, who is the light of the world, filled you with light so that you can illuminate the darkness. It doesn't really matter where that darkness is, only that you illuminate it with your light. That's what Jesus did. He was a carpenter by trade. I can only imagine that he hung out with other carpenters building things and talking about what types of wood work best for building patios and gazebos and things like that. Jesus was a real person who encountered real life scenarios. He didn't have to go out of his way to find some darkness; he just shined where he was.

LIGHT WITHIN THE GAME

Even though I don't want to be like Jonah, sometimes I'm jealous of him. Let's be serious--Jonah had it pretty easy don't you think? Whereas I spend much of my time watching, waiting, and wondering what I'm supposed to do with myself, God directly told Jonah – *go to Nineveh.*

Sometimes life seems like a jigsaw puzzle; you've got a certain number of pieces and your trying to figure out how all the pieces fit together. One thing Bonnie taught me is that you've only got a certain number of days, so you need to spend them wisely.

I often think that if I knew what God wanted me to do I would surely do it, but that's not usually the case. And so I pray and think and wait, and ask and wonder and wait. It has occurred to me on numerous occasions that a person could spend their whole life waiting and never being, but maybe Jon stumbled upon the answer to that dilemma in the garage in Afghanistan; darkness prevailed until he found the light and instantly the wait was over.

That's how I felt last summer when I saw the Adidas commercial during the World Cup. *ONE GAME* that closes shops, schools and cities; stops wars; fuels nations; breaks borders, builds heroes; crushes dreams; answers prayers; and changes the world.

I didn't cry because soccer is the greatest game that answers all of life's questions, heals its hurts, or solves its problems. I cried because I realized that even though I'm not a pastor, Bible scholar, teacher, or theologian, I am a light-bearer in one of the most influential arenas anywhere; sports.

One game changing everything.

Maybe not so much the game but your light within the game.

EIGHT

Glorious Reunification

EIGHT

Glorious Reunification

Political science is not my thing, but borders perturb me.

My work takes me all over the world, so I know
what crossing borders can entail: passports and photos and
paperwork and immunizations and, sometimes, exorbitant
amounts of money. I know borders.

A few years ago my soccer team was playing in Aquba, the
southernmost city in Jordan. As we were there in the summer,
it was really hot. Actually, it was so hot that our game wasn't
allowed to kick off until eleven p.m. The following day our
team was free to do what we wanted, so a few of us decided to
hang out at a beach on the Red Sea. It wasn't the nicest beach
I'd ever been to, but the idea of hanging out by the Red Sea all
day was compelling enough to keep us there.

At one point my friend Tom, a goalkeeper, decided it
would be awesome to swim from Aquba to Israel. Looking
across the Red Sea towards the land on the other side, Tom said,

"How cool would it be if we swam over there, hung out for a while, and then swam back?"

I had to admit that it was a pretty cool idea. Apparently no one else agreed. The only dummy Tom successfully convinced to attempt the feat was me.

I'm not sure how far it is from Aquba to Israel, but when you're standing on the shore looking across the sea it seems close. We figured it would take ten or fifteen minutes at the most, so we went for it.

I regret that decision.

I think we had been swimming for about half an hour when I noticed a speedboat in the distance. I didn't think much of it until I noticed it was racing straight towards Tom and me. There were seven men in the boat. As they got closer we could hear them yelling in Arabic. It wasn't until they had nearly run us over in the water that I realized we were in trouble.

Given my obvious deficiency in Arabic, I'm not sure what the men in the boat were saying. But their wild gesticulation and vociferous manner of expression definitely conveyed the impression that something was wrong. I'm fairly certain that all of them were pointing machine guns at us, but the stress of that event could be clouding my memory. I'm fairly certain though.

I remember trying to explain our well-intentioned swim to the seven men in the speedboat as I treaded water, simultaneously attempting to keep my hands above my head.

That experience was strangely comparable to the lifeguard test I took when I was sixteen. Among other tasks, we had to tread water while holding a brick out of the water for five minutes. On the other hand, the lifeguard instructor never threatened to end the students' lives if we dropped our bricks in the pool. And another thing . . . when have you ever heard of a lifeguard rescuing a drowning brick from a pool?

In any case, it was obvious that the seven men in the speedboat weren't buying what we were selling that day. Our options were limited; swim back to Aquba or be gunned down in the open waters of the Red Sea. Needless to say, we swam.

One Voice, Not Many

I realize now that we should have thought through that Red Sea swim more carefully before we started. Our problem wasn't so much the seven men screaming Arabic obscenities as they pointed their AK-47's at our heads; it was the border they were protecting. No one enters Israel without the proper documentation, even if they're swimming in.

I get it, I do. Borders exist for a reason, but that wasn't always the case. It seems to me that it won't always be the case either.

Actually, Genesis, the "book of beginnings," describes a time in human history when borders didn't exist at all. There was no France or Belgium or Senegal or Colombia. China made no distinction from neighboring Mongolia; the United States was not concerned about illegal immigrants, aliens, or the Office of Homeland Security either.

No, Genesis records a period in human history when everyone was fairly similar, or at least they weren't differentiated by the more recent concept of the sovereign nation-state. Genesis says that "the whole world had one language and a common speech."[111]

Can you imagine that?

What if everyone spoke the same language today? I looked this figure up on Wikipedia, so I'm fairly certain it's accurate . . . but they suggest there are 6,912 different languages in the world and 39,491 more dialects within those languages. Linguists can spend their entire lives attempting to master the nuances of just a few languages, never mind 6,912!

Yet there was a time when everyone spoke the same language. There were not many languages, but *the whole world had one language and a common speech*. Interestingly, *one language* and *common speech* pertained to borders as well.

I'm certainly not a Hebrew scholar, but apparently the writer of Genesis originally used the Hebrew words *saphah* and *dabar* to describe what is often translated to mean *one language* and *common speech* in English.

Saphah, one language.

Dabar, common speech.

In considering the voice of the people of Genesis it is valuable to note the other English translations of those same Hebrew words. While saphah does translate to mean one language it can also mean *speech, shore, bank, brink, brim, side, edge, BORDER, or binding*. Similarly, *dabar* means *speech*, but it can also be a singular *word*, or in its plural form, *speaking*.

Here's the point we should probably consider: there was a time when *the whole world had one language and a common speech*, but it just so happens that the whole world simultaneously had one *side, edge,* or *border* as well. I suppose that one border could just as easily be interpreted as no border at all, depending on your perspective.

I don't think it's any stretch to say that the author of Genesis was trying to tell us that there was a time in human history when the whole world had one border and everyone spoke the same language. So what happened? Why do we now have 6,912 languages, 39,491 dialects, and over 200 recognized countries? In other words, what's the deal with all this separation?

Casting Crowns

The last book of the Bible, Revelation, is full of grand imagery and wonderful ideas of things to come. The word pictures presented of this book are so grandiose that a friend once told me he thought the author had spent one too many nights out on the town with the Cheshire Cat from *Alice in Wonderland*. Regardless, Revelation is an amazing book filled with profound biblical truth.

At one point in Revelation's tale of glorious imagery, it is foretold that a time will come when all people will bow before God's throne and remove the crowns they are wearing on their heads. All will cast their crowns before the throne and with one voice proclaim God's greatness. As the people congregate at God's throne they will all be chanting and singing:

> *Worthy, O Master! Yes, our God!*
> *Take the glory! the honor! the power!*
> *You created it all;*
> *It was created because you wanted it.*[112]

Revelation predicts a day that is coming when the many voices will become one, when all people will cast their crowns of personal glory at God's feet and proclaim his greatness above everything else. On that day we will no longer be separated by language or dialect, and borders will cease to exist. One day that will be the case. In the meantime . . . it's not.

Not Made to Babel

In the meantime, our nature deems us a people who love our own voice. In Chapter One we talked about the people from Genesis who said to themselves, "Come, let us build ourselves a city, with a tower that reaches to the heavens." Do you think they cared more about the city or the tower? I don't think they cared much about either, to tell you the truth. The masses described in Genesis conspired to make a name for themselves; they were a people who loved their own voice and they wanted that to be known everywhere.

But here's what happened.

At one time, the whole Earth spoke the same language. It so happened that as they moved out of the east, they came upon a plain in the land of Shinar and settled down. They said to one another, "Come, let's make bricks and fire them well." They used brick for stone and tar for mortar. Then they said, "Come, let's build ourselves a city and a tower that reaches Heaven. *Let's make ourselves* famous so we won't be scattered here and there across the Earth."

God came down to look over the city and the tower those people had built.

God took one look and said, "One people, one language; why, this is only a first step. No telling what they'll come up with next—they'll stop at nothing! Come, we'll go down and garble their speech so they won't understand each other." Then God scattered them from there all over the world. And they had to quit

building the city. That's how it came to be called Babel,
because there God turned their language into "babble."
From there God scattered them all over the world.[113]

From antiquity the masses have shared the same goal: me.
Not so much me in respect to *me* the author of this book or *me* a
guy who's not you, but rather ME, the one who's different from
everyone else and wants the world to know it—ME. That was
man's original problem, and it continues to be our problem today.

Inherently we are a people who care more about us then
we do about *them*. Though created by God in the image of
God for God, we are a people who live for us. Whether you
acknowledge that or not, it's true.

That may be our nature, but it doesn't have to be our
disposition. As we've said before, we were created for one
game, but now there are two: God's and ours. Remember, God
created the grandest, most important, coolest game of all games,
like the Super Bowl, Rugby World Cup Final, NBA Finals
and World Cup of soccer all rolled into one. Adam and Eve's
decision to take their ball and play elsewhere didn't affect God's
Game of all Games from proceeding as planned but, as we've
discussed, it did open the door for choice.

At Babel one voice became many, and subsequently,
one border became many as well. The original people had *one
language and a common speech*. Remember what Wikipedia told

us? There are now 6,912 languages and 39,491 dialects on our planet, scattered throughout over 200 countries, maintained by borders that separate me from you and vice versa.

But while Babel caused separation, God is calling everything back towards unity.

One Goal: God

Speaking through the Old Testament prophet Zephaniah, God foretold a day when separation would be no more. Zephaniah wrote, "In the end I will turn things around for the people. I'll give them a language undistorted, unpolluted, Words to address GOD in worship and, united, to serve me with their shoulders to the wheel. . . . All my scattered, exiled people will come home with offerings for worship."[114]

Theologians call Zephaniah's prediction the "great unification." On that day of great unification, national borders, languages, dialects, and separation will cease to exist; everyone will be unified in God, for God's glory.

That seems right to me.

Sure, separation rules the day. We see that clearly in an event like the World Cup of soccer and the many nations and peoples participating—but that was never God's intention. Over and over throughout the Bible God repeats his mantra for unity—all things were created by him and for him. After all, that is what the real you is all about: God.

Once upon a time everyone had one language and a common speech. Everyone was united by a common purpose. Everyone shared the same theme: God. When I look at the world today, with all of our disputes and anger and opposition towards one another, I often wonder what life was like in the days before Babel. Sometimes I long for a world like that, a world not separated by national identity or linguistic ability. Practically, I have no idea what that looks like, but God does, and actually, it's where we are all heading.

From Babel forward everything, including you and me, has been moving back towards God's ultimate goal: God.

Though Adam and Eve initiated the really small game for personal glory, and God has allowed for a choice between his game and our own, the day is coming in which that will no longer be an option. Paul writes about the day when everyone will be unified in the worship of God. He says, "At the name of Jesus every knee should bow, in heaven and on earth and under the earth, and every tongue confess that Jesus Christ is Lord."[115] This is a wonderful promise of Scripture, but its purpose is often overlooked.

There is a reason that every knee will bow and every tongue confess that Jesus Christ is Lord. Paul is quite clear in his expression of the reason: *to the glory of God the Father.*[116]

Paul communicated the same message to the early God-followers in Rome: "From him and through him and to him are all things."[117] This has always been God's goal for us. Optometrists, bellmen, prosecutors, third-grade teachers, presidential candidates, servers at McDonald's, library clerks, highway patrol officers, sportsmen--everyone and everything is moving back towards a glorious reunification of purpose: God's glory.

God Thankers

The realization that all things are moving back towards God's glory thoroughly excites me, but simultaneously it makes the little hairs on the back of my neck stand at attention with fear and trembling.

Several years ago I came across a Bible story that made me think about my life and my sporting career. It also made me think about other sportsmen.

One of Jesus' closest friends heard Jesus share a story about God's passion to be glorified, illustrated through people who will approach God when their life on earth has finished.

Matthew records Jesus saying this:

> "Knowing the correct password—saying 'Master, Master,' for instance—isn't going to get you anywhere with me [God]. What is required is serious obedience— doing what my Father wills. I can see it now—at the Final Judgment thousands strutting up to me and saying, 'Master, we preached the Message, we bashed the demons, our God-sponsored projects had everyone

talking.' And do you know what I am going to say? 'You missed the boat. All you did was use me to make yourselves important. You don't impress me one bit. You're out of here."[118]

That really made me think.

What if you came to the end of your life on earth and God said to you: *You missed the boat. All you did was use me to make yourselves important.*

I suppose this story could pertain to any number of the billions of people who have been involved in this thing called humanity, but let's suppose it's all about you. God may or may not say that to me, your brother, or the girl you just passed on your way to Starbucks, but what if he says that to you?

I told you my purpose.

I told you my passion.

I told you how you could participate, but you missed the boat. All you did was use me to make yourself important.

It would be pretty awful to hear God say that, especially if you thought you had been on board with his plan.

I fear that far too many sportsmen confess Jesus with their lips but deny him by their lifestyle. That might not be a conscious objective, but it happens.

Sometimes I watch SportsCenter to fill in and catch up on sports news. When sportsmen are interviewed after a big game or at a special function, we often hear them make comments like, "First of all, I'd like to thank Jesus. . . ." Sometimes they point to the sky, shake their heads, and they say things like, "God made this all possible. I couldn't have done it without God and my teammates."

When I hear comments like that I think to myself, *That's so nice, they're thanking Jesus.* But I have a great fear that many of these sportsmen think they're going to strut into heaven someday in their team-issued kit with their rings on their fingers and their highlight films in their backpacks and announce, "Praise God, I'm here!"

I fear they may miss the boat before they get there.

Don't get me wrong. I'm guilty too. I've done the same thing. I've been one of those post-game Jesus-thankers. That's what scares me.

Now, I think Jesus probably does appreciate being recognized in many circumstances, but the apostle Paul cautioned, "Do not be deceived: God cannot be mocked. A man reaps what he sows."[119] It's one thing to point to the sky and say "God gets the glory" after a soccer game; it's an entirely different thing to live for the glory of God.

I don't want to hear Jesus say: *You missed the boat. All you did was use me to make yourself important.*

Dumb Student

The great news is that our separation and opposing purposes are daily moving back towards a glorious reunification with God. Though we are a people who love our own voice and aspire to make ourselves known, God created each of us for the same purpose--at all times, in all places, in all circumstances, and all things.

God has one goal: God.

If you are anything like me you probably forget that. Or maybe it's not so much that you forget it as that your vision for God's glory in your life becomes convoluted at times. I suppose from God's perspective the "boat" is unchanging; the real question is whether you're on it or you're not.

I had a professor in university who was scarier than Genghis Khan on steroids. Granted, he was no more than five feet tall and 110 pounds soaking wet, but he was a scary dude, trust me. On one particular occasion this professor was instructing our class on the specifics for an upcoming exam. Near the end of the class, a kid in the front of the lecture hall raised his hand. I knew immediately that he was making a mistake. Regardless, he kept his hand raised until the professor noticed him.

For some reason the student's question perturbed him. In fact, he was so annoyed that his entire face scrunched up like a shar-pei puppy I once saw on Animal Planet. The professor proceeded to squeal audibly, making a noise similar to what I imagine K-9s hear when their master blows on a silent dog whistle. After several minutes, and decibels, of the awkward squealing noise, the professor finally said, *"You are a dumb student!"*

It was a huge class, but no one moved or said anything.

The professor looked at the boy and said, *"I tell you all the answers; now you ask a dumb question!"*

I never saw that student after that.

I've not seen that professor since university, but I always think about his comment: I tell you all the answers.

At times I wonder if God feels anything like that scary university professor.

It's like Paul wrote after meeting Jesus on the road to Damascus, "There is only one God, the Father, who created everything, and we exist for him."[120]

But so often we don't.

We move through the many details of our lives with knowledge of God and his glory, yet with an even stronger commitment to our own.

For many of us, life provides an opportunity to make a name for ourselves. We try not to think about things to come, but when we do, we find comfort in a momentary acknowledgement of God.

I wonder if God looks at his creation sometimes and thinks to himself, "Dumb students! I told them all the answers!"

God has one goal: God.

To Who

I returned from Brazil recently. It was a great trip. I hung out with some amazing people, sampled the food of that region, and even danced the samba. It's a bold statement, but I would be willing to say I *loved* my trip to Brazil. Yet, as much as I love any journey, I love coming home even more.

Most often when I'm traveling outside of the United States I return through one of two cities, Newark or Houston. I get off the plane, walk to customs, stand in a line, and when my turn arrives I step up to the counter and greet the Homeland Security agent. The agent usually has a question or two about the purpose of my trip, but it's nothing compared to other borders I cross as an American.

On this particular occasion I returned from Brazil through Newark, New Jersey. I went through the standard routine, and just before the agent stamped my passport for re-entry he looked up, smiled, and said, "Welcome home."

At the moment we live in a world defined by nations and languages and dialects and people groups. These things separate us. Yet, despite our current separation, all of creation is moving back towards the glory of God. We are moving towards a day when with one voice we will proclaim *together* that God is great above all things and worthy of all praise.

In the meantime we're on a journey towards home.

If you're a sportsman it might be helpful to view your journey as a competition in which all of humanity is participating. Though everyone is competing, the competition has nothing to do with me versus you. It's not about my team versus your team or us against them. The Grand Competition of life is always for *glory*; my glory versus God's.

One day the competition will be over; only God's glory will remain, and all of creation will proclaim, "Holy, holy, holy is the Lord Almighty; the whole earth is full of his glory."[121]

We aren't home yet, so the question remains: *To who?*

You choose.

- SDG

1   1 Corinthians 9:24 (NLT).

2   "History of Athletes." Google Answers. Web. 26 Aug. 2010. <http://answers.google.com/answers/threadview/id/493779.html>.

3   Online Etymology Dictionary. Web. 26 Aug. 2010. <http://www.etymonline.com/index.php?term=athlete>.

4   "Sportsman" is the common term used today but the term "athlete" originally referred to any sportsman or sports competitor.

5   Fox Sports. Web 26 Aug. 2010. http://www.msn.foxsports.com/nba/story/5314632.

6   Luke 9:25 (The Message).

7   1 Corinthians 8:6 (NLT).

8   Colossians 1:16 (The Message).

9   Genesis 1:27 (NLT).

10   Genesis 3:1 (NLT).

11   Random House Unabridged Dictionary, © Random House, Inc. 2006.

12   Isaiah 6:3 (NIV).

13   Rob Bell, Velvet Elvis: Repainting the Christian Faith. Zondervan, 2006, p. 77.

14   Isaiah 48:11 (NIV).

15   Genesis 11:4 (NIV)

16   Isaiah 6:3 (NIV)

17   Ecclesiastes 1:16-17 (NLT).

18   See Ecclesiastes 2:8-9.

19   Ecclesiastes 3:11 (NIV).

20   Psalms 42:1 (NLT).

21   Blaise Pascal.

22   Ecclesiastes 2:25.

23   Ephesians 2:10 (NLT).

24   Jeremiah 29:11 (The Message).

25   See Jeremiah 29:11.

26   Max Lucado, It's Not About Me. Thomas Nelson, Inc., 2004, p. 28.

27   Isaiah 43:6-7 (NIV, italics mine).

28   John 3:16 (The Message).

29   I Corinthians 10:31 (NIV).

30   Exodus 3:4-14 (The Message).

31   Louie Giglio, I am not but I know I AM. Hodder and Stroughton, 2006. A more exhaustive look at this concept can be found in Louie Giglio's book. I'd like to thank Louie for his seminal work in what he calls "the story of God" and how that work has shaped much of my thinking on this topic.

32   Philippians 4:13 (NASB, emphasis mine).

33   Romans 8:37 (NIV, emphasis mine).

34   Psalm 60:12 (NLT, emphasis mine).

35 "Evel Knievel Quotes, Sayings and Quotations." 450,000 Famous Quotes - Inspirational Quotes - Friendship & Life Quotes - Famous Sayings & Proverbs - Great Quotes! Web. 26 Aug. 2010. <http://www.great-quotes.com/cgi-bin/viewquotes.cgi?action=search&Movie=Evel Knievel>.

36 Proverbs 16:18 (The Message).

37 Random House Unabridged Dictionary, © Random House, Inc. 2006.

38 "Evel Knievel Quotes." Famous Quotes and Quotations at BrainyQuote. Web. 26 Aug. 2010. <http://www.brainyquote.com/quotes/authors/e/evel_knievel_2.html>.

39 Luke 9:25 (The Message).

40 John Piper, Let the nations be glad. Baker Publishing Group, 2010, p.225.

41 Romans 9:17 (NIV).

42 Isaiah 53:6 (NLT).

43 I John 2:15 (The Message)

44 Daniel 4:1-3 (NIV).

45 Daniel 4:25 (NLT)

46 Daniel 4:24-26 (NLT, emphasis mine).

47 See Romans 1:20 and Romans 2:5-6.

48 Daniel 4:34-35 (NLT).

49 Daniel 4:37 (NIV).

50   Luke 17:33 (NIV).

51   Matthew 10:39 (The Message).

52   Mia Hamm.

53   Vince Lombardi.

54   George Steinbrenner.

55   Philippians 2:9 (The Message).

56   Stevens, Dana. "TNT's Evel Knievel Snoozefest. - By Dana Stevens." Slate Magazine. Web. 26 Aug. 2010. <http://www.slate.com/id/2104564/>.

57   Daniel 4:27 (NIV).

58   Usain Bolt is the current World Record holder in the 100 and 200 meter sprints. He is currently the "fastest man on earth."

59   1 Corinthians 9:24 (NLT).

60   Psalm 50:10b, 12b (NLT).

61   1 Corinthians 8:6 (NLT).

62   Max Lucado, It's Not About Me. Thomas Nelson, Inc., 2004, p. 6.

63   Although motivation does differ between men and women, women tend to value participation as much as, or more than, winning or losing. This assertion is directly taken from the 1999 Master's Thesis study entitled Motivational Differences Between Men and Women Competing in Collegiate Soccer by Aaron Tredway.

64 I would not disagree that many people in Western culture maintain a relativistic worldview. Yet, within this assertion I am addressing what I believe to be the majority-held belief system.

65 1 Samuel 9:2 (NLT).

66 1 Samuel16:6 (NLT).

67 1 Samuel16:7 (NIV).

68 Sermon Illustrations. Web. 26 Aug. 2010. <http://www.sermonillustrations.com/a-z/s/singlemindedness.htm>.

69 Thomas de Zengotita, Mediated: How the Media Shapes Your World and the Way You Live in It. Bloomsbury, 2006, p. 117.

70 Before you jump to any conclusions about what I am saying, bear in mind that I am the star of a MySpace account too.

71 Stephen R. Covey, The 7 Habits of Highly Effective People. Free Press, a Division of Simon and Schuster, 2004, p. 23.

72 Ibid., p. 29.

73 "Starbucks." Wikipedia, the Free Encyclopedia. Web. 27 Aug. 2010. <http://en.wikipedia.org/wiki/Starbucks>.

74 Os Guinness has profoundly impacted and shaped my thinking as it pertains to matters of worldview. If you are interested in worldview give yourself a treat and read Rising to the Call by Os Guinness (Thomas Nelson, Inc., 2008)

75   1 Corinthians 6:12 (NIV).

76   See Esther 4:6-14.

77   T.S. Eliot.

78   See I Peter 4:10

79   Matthew 7:3 (The Message).

80   Romans 3:22-23 (NIV).

81   Colossians 1:21 (NIV).

82   1 Timothy 19 (NIV).

83   John 10:10 (NLT).

84   John 10:10 (The Message).

85   Donald Miller, Searching For God Knows What. Thomas Nelson, Inc., p. 13.

86   I Peter 2:9 (NIV)

87   Ephesians 1:4-5 (NIV).

88   Ephesians 1:4-5 (NIV).

89   1 Corinthians 10:31 (NIV).

90   Romans 11:36 (NLT).

91   Matthew 12:30 (NIV).

92   George Orwell, The Complete Works of George Orwell, Vol. 1, "Pacifism and War." Secker and Warburg, 1998, p. 396

93   Mark 11:17 (NIV).

94   1 Peter 2:10 (NIV).

95   1 Corinthians 1:27 (NIV).

96   As seen in the 1984 release of the film "Amadeus"

97   Romans 12:1-2 (The Message)

98   Quoted in: Os Guinness, The Call: Finding and Fulfilling
      the Central Purpose of Your Life. Thomas Nelson, 2007,
      p. 122

99   1 Corinthians 1:27 (NIV).

100   Nelson Mandela is the famous South African apartheid
      revolutionary who has spent his life in opposition to
      racial discrimination and social barriers. Mandela has
      been a bold advocate for sport as a medium of racial
      reconciliation and unification.

101   Psalm 103:15 (NIV).

102   Jonah 1:1-2 (The Message).

103   Jonah 2:8 (NIV).

104   Matthew 5:14 (NIV).

105   Matthew 5:14-15 (The Message).

106   John 8:12 (NLT, emphasis mine).

107   John 1:1,14 (NIV).

108   Os Guiness, The Call: Finding and Fulfilling the Central
      Purpose of Your Life. Thomas Nelson, Inc., 2003, p. 31.

109   Romans 12:4-5 (NIV).

110   Romans 12:6 (The Message).

111   Genesis 11:1 (NIV).

112   Revelation 4:11 (The Message).

113   Genesis 11:1-9 (The Message, italics mine).

114   Zephaniah 3:9-11 (The Message).

115 Philippians 2:10-11a (NIV).

116 Philippians 2:11b (NIV).

117 Romans 11:36 (NIV).

118 Matthew 7:21-23 (The Message).

119 Galatians 6:7 (NIV).

120 I Corinthians 8:6 (NLT).

121 Isaiah 6:3 (NIV).